KALE & CARAMEL

Recipes for Body, Heart, and Table

Lily Diamond

ATRIA PAPERBACK

New York   London   Toronto   Sydney   New Delhi

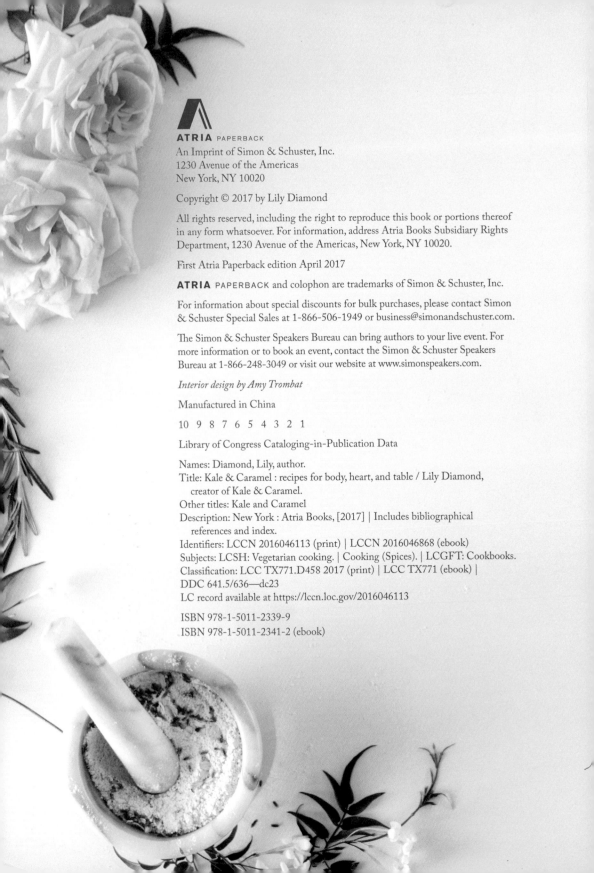

ATRIA PAPERBACK

An Imprint of Simon & Schuster, Inc.
1230 Avenue of the Americas
New York, NY 10020

First Atria Paperback edition April 2017

ATRIA PAPERBACK and colophon are trademarks of Simon & Schuster, Inc.

For information about special discounts for bulk purchases, please contact Simon
& Schuster Special Sales at 1-866-506-1949 or business@simonandschuster.com.

The Simon & Schuster Speakers Bureau can bring authors to your live event. For
more information or to book an event, contact the Simon & Schuster Speakers
Bureau at 1-866-248-3049 or visit our website at www.simonspeakers.com.

Interior design by Amy Trombat

Manufactured in China

10 9 8 7 6 5 4 3 2 1

Library of Congress Cataloging-in-Publication Data

Names: Diamond, Lily, author.
Title: Kale & Caramel : recipes for body, heart, and table / Lily Diamond,
    creator of Kale & Caramel.
Other titles: Kale and Caramel
Description: New York : Atria Books, [2017] | Includes bibliographical
    references and index.
Identifiers: LCCN 2016046113 (print) | LCCN 2016046868 (ebook)
Subjects: LCSH: Vegetarian cooking. | Cooking (Spices). | LCGFT: Cookbooks.
Classification: LCC TX771.D458 2017 (print) | LCC TX771 (ebook) |
DDC 641.5/636—dc23
LC record available at https://lccn.loc.gov/2016046113

ISBN 978-1-5011-2339-9
ISBN 978-1-5011-2341-2 (ebook)

*Cooking is like love. It should be entered
into with abandon or not at all.*

HARRIET VAN HORNE, 1956

Contents

HERBS

7 SAGE *133*

Persimmon Bites with Pomegranate Molasses & Crispy Sage Leaves 134

Black Bean & Sage-Roasted Butternut Quesadillas 137

Creamy Fresh Corn Polenta with Sage, Parmesan & Crispy Shallots 140

Sage Salted Caramel Ice Cream 143

Citrus Sage Tonic (Vegan) 146

8 THYME *149*

Braised Radicchio, Nectarine & Burrata Flatbread 150

Thyme-Scented Plum & Arugula Salad with Honey Hazelnut Clusters 153

Roasted Tomato Soup with Thyme-Crusted Grilled Cheese 157

Fig & Honeyed Thyme Ricotta Galette 159

Lemon Thyme Vanilla Bean Sorbet 163

Pomegranate & Thyme Spritzer (Vegan) 165

FLOWERS

9 LAVENDER *173*

Butter Lettuce with Herbes de Provence Vinaigrette (Vegan) 174

Mini Lavender Blueberry No-Bake Goat Cheesecakes 177

Honey Lavender Ice Cream with Lemon Curd Swirl 180

Lavender Honey Lemonade 183

Lavender Sea Salt Beach Hair Spritz 186

Lavender Oat Milk Bath 189

Night Night Oil 190

10 JASMINE *193*

Matcha Coconut Cream Parfaits with Jasmine Shortbread (Vegan) 195

Jasmine Cacao Nib Ice Cream with Dark Chocolate Magic Shell 197

Fresh Jasmine Honey 200

Jasmine Cucumber Water (Vegan) 203

Jasmine Facial Oil, Two Ways 204

11 ROSE *207*

Cumin & Rose Roasted Cauliflower with Vinegar-Soaked Currants 208

Peach & Pistachio Galettes with Rose Whipped Cream 211

Chocolate Chia Mousse with Cardamom Rose Coco Whip (Vegan) 214

Pink Grapefruit, Cucumber & Rose Skin Quencher (Vegan) 217

Watermelon Rose Elixir (Vegan) 221

Honey Rose Facial Cleanser 222

Cucumber Rose Petal Mask 225

12 ORANGE BLOSSOM *227*

Carrot, Feta & Pistachio Salad with Orange Blossom Toss 228

Orange Blossom Pistachio Milk 231

Fig & Orange Blossom Yogurt Tarts 235

Coconut, Hibiscus & Blood Orange Blossom Slushies 237

Citrus Blossom Sugar Brightening Scrub 240

Full Moon Blossom Oil 242

Introduction

This book, and the food and art and plants that live in it, was born out of great longing. From my earliest memories, I was the longing kind—I longed for friends, I longed for boys to like me, I longed for my skin to be darker, my waist to be thinner, my parents to be more normal, my self to be cooler. I longed my way into college and, after that, I longed my way into being in love. I longed myself into jobs and spiritual frenzies and entire personas that were not really me. And when my mother got sick and died, then, too, I longed for things to be different. I longed for family. I longed not to feel fractured. I longed to feel some kind of home, sometime again.

I longed for love.

And then, one day, I longed to stop longing. In the wake of utter exhaustion— the mental and physical depletion of grief, spiritual seeking, and emotional hunger—the longing fell away. Finally, I didn't want anything outside of myself. Instead, I began the work of stripping myself down to be made anew. I wanted to be made of freedom, not fear. Action instead of tears. Wildness instead of longing.

It is said that the mind will only truly change when it grows so weary of itself it cannot stand to repeat its machinations for even one more moment. And so it was with me, that the heavier the grief weighed on me, the more I wanted to be free. For years, I let grief subsume me in its shadowy net, allowed feeling to run through me like water. I let myself go through every stage Elisabeth Kübler-Ross outlined for the one who grieves. I wrote dark poetry. I railed against the injustice of having a heart that was broken in one half by the loss of my mother, my best friend, and broken in another by the love I thought I'd be with for always. Though my heart has broken many times since, the first strike—and my commitment to emerge from it with some semblance of wholeness—was enough to birth a transcendent will to change. To stop longing.

Because when the heart is broken so many times, it either breaks, once and for all, or, in its exquisitely shattered state, it becomes unbreakable.

What came when I stopped longing was being, pure and wild. Being with food that nourished me. Being with plants and flowers that healed by virtue of their very existence, their wildness. Being, no matter how much my heart hurt.

"There's rosemary, that's for remembrance; pray you, love, remember," Ophelia says as she presses the herb into her brother's palm. Shakespeare knew: The way we remember our humanity is by knowing our relationship to the world around us, to the plants that sustain us.

The herbs and flowers that populate the chapters of this book were each critical elements in a world, a life, that was about being more than longing. Rose soothed a dozen broken hearts, lavender tamed my mind and fought away tears, oregano cleared out emotional detritus, fennel softened the calcifications that kept me hard, jasmine took my breath away, and basil gave it back again. Rosemary grounded my feet on the earth, thyme strengthened my resolve, and mint kept me awake. Orange blossom sweetened my tongue when cilantro reminded me of bitterness, and sage kept clear watch over my heart's truth.

These plants are my pulse. They are my way back, again and again, to the wild.

I pray you, love, remember.

Biodynamic nourishment

Somewhere along the way, eating beautiful and feeling beautiful took separate paths. We shop in different areas of the store for our food and our body care, when, in truth, feeding our stomachs, our skin, and our hearts is one and the same. In creating Kale & Caramel, I wanted to resurrect this back-to-the-earth belief with a modern twist: an ease and effortlessness in caring for yourself, in living in right relationship with the earth, in eating foods that will make you feel as vibrant as that blackberry basil healing mask makes you look.

The name Kale & Caramel came from my desire to express healthfulness and a sense of luxuriant, delicious play, and over the years it has become a 360-degree lifestyle approach: a means of living in a biodynamic household. Many of the ingredients used transcend the boundary between food and body product, introducing a seamless kind of lifestyle integrity. What you use in the kitchen should be pure enough to apply to your skin. And what you slather on your body should be pure enough to eat. This closed circuit of nourishment will naturally reconnect you with a way of living that is tactile, sensorial, and closer to the earth.

My biodynamic approach to kitchen and body came from years of tutelage under the great open sky and land of Maui, from the wisdom of my mother—a consummate herbalist and aromatherapist—and from the freedom I gave myself to play with food as often and as enthusiastically as I wanted.

I first learned to communicate with the plants on walks through the garden, held in my mother's arms. I learned by leaf and petal, by scent and texture and taste. From that safe nook of mother-warmth, my legs wrapped around her rib cage, her hands showed me a world full of leaves that cured burns, flowers that eased anxiety, and foods that healed systemic imbalances. I said yes. Yes, I would explore. Yes, I would live here,

among these plants that could teach, delight, and nourish. Yes, I would learn.

My mother was an exacting purist, and a complete and utter health nut. She grew her own herbs and flowers to infuse and distill, and spent decades living the pre-hipster definition of farm-to-table. Her first book, *Living with the Flowers*, was published before I was born. Together, my parents joined a kind of commune called the Alive Tribe, into which I was born in Bolinas, California, in 1983.

We left the Tribe and moved to Maui when I was two. My earliest memories are of salt, wet sand, emerald strands of luminescent seaweed, and shining black lava rock. Ocean. Sky. The scent of plumeria. Clouds. Damp skin and refracting sunlight.

Every day, my parents gardened together in the abundant grounds my mother designed on our mountainside property. We had three acres, much of it not landscaped; above and below us was ranch land with roaming cattle, and to the side was Maui's only vineyard. I grew up understanding that food came from the land, and that it was my responsibility to help care for that land. My early Waldorf education integrated gardening, composting, baking bread, and eating copious amounts of nutritional yeast into my daily routine.

Though we ate out occasionally, we had the luxury of living on land that was generous and good to our bodies. We grew most of the fruits and vegetables we ate: apple bananas; Surinam cherries; Tahitian limes; Meyer lemons; at least three kinds of avocados; strawberry papayas; yellow, purple, and Jamaican lilikoi (passion fruit); tangelos; navel oranges; tangerines; every kind of lettuce and herb you can think of; carrots; beets—and my favorite—a pomegranate tree.

When I flew off to college at Yale, my mother sent me with a healing kit full of naturopathic and homeopathic remedies for any ailment that I might encounter. I quickly became a kind of in-dorm apothecary, channeling my mother's holistic health knowledge as best I could. I prescribed lavender essential oil for sleeplessness, echinacea for colds, and peppermint for nausea.

Just a year after I graduated, my mother was diagnosed with advanced-stage cancer. The consummate healer, the one everyone turned to for natural health wisdom, was now in crisis herself. I returned to Maui to help my father care for her, and a year and a half post-diagnosis, she passed away.

Suddenly, the person who had always nourished me was gone, the template for the world as I knew it knocked out of place. In the years that followed, writing became a refuge, as did creative time in the kitchen. In both places, she was ever present.

In 2012, at the urging of friends and mentors, I started Kale & Caramel. The blog quickly became a locus for my dual loves of writing and playing with food. It is, undeniably, my happy place—a way for me to nourish both others and myself in the way my mother once fed me.

Today, my life in Los Angeles is full of city streets, urban farmers' markets, gridlock, and the weight of human distance from the land. I wake up most mornings longing for dirt, for ocean, for a place where I might orient myself back to the plants. This is one way: a deep dive into the potency of fresh herbs and flowers that impart flavor and healing qualities into all they touch. Tokens of freshness, of earth, of wildness, at home with me. No matter where I live.

Food for all five senses

Orange blossom pistachio milk. Thyme-scented plum and arugula salad. Lavender blueberry cheesecake. Before you write off my food preferences as more annoyingly highbrow than Blair Waldorf at a sample sale, let me explain.

Every leaf, every petal, has a code. Like any good html, that code unfolds and takes its intended action in the body and mind when given the space to do so. So it is with the plants that populate these pages. They are your allies, ready to take you back to the wildness of the senses at any moment.

The relationship between scent and taste is particularly deep. Scent adds a significant dimension to taste, synesthesia-style, and dictates our ability to tease apart and experience complex flavors.

On the most basic level, the smell of a food is carried through our nasal passages when we chew, inextricably linking taste and aroma. On a more complex level, adding uniquely fragranced elements to food (like lemongrass and basil to coconut ice cream) transforms the experience of eating, as well as the flavor.

Scent and memory have a strong scientific bond in the brain: Scent elicits memory more intensely than any other sense. When I'm eating a rose caramel from my favorite chocolatier in San Francisco, I'm transported to a rose garden in France on a hot July night. Potent. Sensual.

The recipes in this book—both those to eat and those to anoint your body—are meant to awaken sensory perception at every level. From learning to select the right produce via sight, smell, and feel to discerning the textures of each ingredient and tasting or applying the final product, every recipe is an opportunity to come alive in a new way.

Though food and body care may seem an unusual pairing, the products we use on our bodies become food for our skin and organs. The body's largest organ is the skin, and anything applied to the skin is immediately absorbed into the body. What beautifies within beautifies without. I keep a jar of raw honey by my sink to use as face wash. I make my own saltwater hair spritz to use post-shower. I slather myself with coconut, almond, and olive oils (and yes, sometimes even butter when I'm making a mess in the kitchen).

Keeping my body, skin, and hair healthy with the same vital nutrients and ingredients I use in the kitchen reminds me, on a daily basis, of my connection to the earth. Its health is my health. My beauty is inextricably related to the beauty and wholeness of the planet.

As I build upon my mother's legacy—using herbs and flowers for culinary and aesthetic pleasure in my own, distinct forms—I find my way out of grief and into a new vitality. A return to wildness.

These recipes offer a nourishment that goes far beyond nutrition: They are a true food for the spirit.

Making aromatics a part of your life

In the kitchen, the category of aromatics is largely composed of herbs and flowers that release, impart, and imbue scent to food. This book is organized by individual aromatics and is designed to show you numerous ways to use each. Many will be familiar to you, and some will be new discoveries. Most of them will be available at your local grocery store. Some of them may be more exotic. The following section provides a guide to sourcing and enjoying the aromatics that are the lifeblood of this book.

Even though eating or applying something like rose water feels fancy, it does not require a well-padded bank account. I have lived my entire adult life as a freelancer without a steady paycheck, and have always found easy ways to incorporate these ingredients into my budget. It's simply a matter of desire. For example: Ordering dried lavender, rose, and jasmine online is just an inexpensive click away if you don't have a local health food store with a bulk section that sells them.

These are ingredients that might take some getting used to, but once you begin enjoying them on a regular basis, you'll find that they're both easy to acquire and easy to use. Using single-source botanical products also means you'll save a huge amount of money on the body and beauty care products you typically purchase.

Gathering a few simple, inexpensive ingredients that you can keep in your pantry for months will transform your skin and your palate. All it takes is making the choice.

Also, something to know about me: I'm impatient. Yes, I like getting all DIY and making my own face wash from honey and rose petals and my own sea salt hair spray, but I also like things easy and fast. This means that even the most seemingly complex recipe in this book is secretly one for the impatient at heart. Don't worry. You've got this.

Finally, a word about where to source herbs and flowers in fresh, dried, and essential oil forms.

WHERE TO GET FRESH HERBS AND FLOWERS

The grocery store

Shockingly, the traditional grocery store closest to me has a far better selection of fresh, locally grown herbs than my local health food store—at much cheaper prices. Which is to say: Almost every grocery store these days has a decent selection of fresh herbs; all you have to do is ask.

Moreover, some grocery stores will carry fresh, pesticide-free lavender.

The farmers' market

Your local farmers' market is a treasure trove. Get to know the farmers and their specialties. You will be richly rewarded with fresh herbs and pesticide-free flowers, like edible lavender and rose.

Make friends with folks who have gardens

They will likely have an abundance of herbs and flowers and will be happy to share.

Find your local community garden

Get out on the streets and scout it, Google it, or ask your neighbors and friends—I promise you that somewhere in your relative vicinity there is a community garden waiting to be discovered. I volunteer at the one near me, and am rewarded graciously with planty extras from the folks who have plots.

Grow your own

Whether you live in a place with abundant outdoor space or in a city apartment with barely enough room for a single houseplant, you can grow herbs and flowers in the comfort of your own home. This is not a gardening book, but I fully empower you to develop your own green thumb, no matter where you live.

WHERE TO GET DRIED HERBS AND FLOWERS, AND FLORAL WATERS

Your local health food store with a bulk section
Many health food stores with bulk sections will sell dried herbs in bulk or in bottles. These same stores may also offer dried lavender, rose, and other flowers in their bulk or spices section. Never hurts to ask.

Almost all grocery stores have a selection of jasmine green tea and rose water, and many specialty grocers will carry orange blossom water. Look for rose and orange blossom waters in the international foods or baking aisles.

Online
These sources all provide a large selection of organic, wild-crafted herbs, flowers, and oils. Many of their products are also available through Amazon.
Mountain Rose Herbs: www.mountainroseherbs.com
Frontier Co-Op: www.frontiercoop.com
Starwest Botanicals: www.starwest-botanicals.com

WHERE TO GET ESSENTIAL OILS

Your local health food store
Many health food stores also sell essential oils.

Your local apothecary shop
Every town has a witchy little shop that sells crystals and moon charts. Find yours. They'll have essential oils, too. Promise.

Online
These sites provide a large selection of organic and wild-crafted essential oils. Many of their products are also available through Amazon. I trust all of these brands.
Mountain Rose Herbs: www.mountainroseherbs.com
Starwest Botanicals: www.starwest-botanicals.com
Young Living: www.youngliving.com
Floracopeia: www.floracopeia.com

Infusions

Oil, honey, sugar, salt

Aromatics are as exquisite infused into base ingredients as they are when used as accents to the recipes that follow. These easy techniques of infusion result in products that can be used for both food and body and beauty treatments, reducing the addition of extra ingredients. For example: Once infused, lavender olive oil performs just as perfectly drizzled over a slice of toast with ricotta and wildflower honey as it does poured into your homemade sea salt hair spritz.

The most important thing to keep in mind when selecting herbs and flowers to infuse is the following: Tender leaves or petals (such as fresh rose, fresh mint, or fresh basil) contain more water than dry-leaved, hardy herbs like rosemary and thyme, so they will infuse differently than dried versions of these plants. Instructions for each follow.

Infused oils

Remember the part where I mentioned I'm not the most patient? There are many ways to infuse oil that take much longer, and involve sunlight and titration and witches' spells and moon-bathing (just kidding). This method is the way around all of that, and will give you a quick-infused, hyper-fragrant oil in mere minutes.

Heating the oil does decrease its shelf life, so make sure to prepare smaller batches of oil and try to use them within two weeks to a month. Hardy fresh herbs like rosemary or dried herbs and flowers should be used with this method—rosemary-infused olive oil is a perennial favorite.

Though you can infuse any oil of your choosing, I primarily use extra-virgin olive oil for cooking, and raw virgin coconut oil and sweet almond oil for body care. Olive and coconut oils can be found in the oils section of your grocery store, and sweet almond oil in the body care area of your local health food store.

2 parts oil of choice

1 part hardy or dried herb or flower of choice

In a medium saucepan, heat the oil over low heat. When it's almost too hot to touch, add the herbs or flowers. Use a silicone spatula or wooden spoon to stir and massage the herbs against the base of the pan in order to release the aromatic oils. Keep over the heat for another 15 to 30 seconds, then remove from the heat. Cool completely, then transfer to a clean, dry glass jar and seal. Let sit for at least a few hours, and up to 48 hours for a stronger infusion.

Strain through cheesecloth and discard the plant material. Store the infused oil in an airtight container, in a cool place out of sunlight.

Infused honey

Honey can be infused with almost anything you like, resulting in a sultry harmony of flavors that complements savory and sweet dishes as beautifully as it does any body and beauty products you can dream up. Because honey is a natural preservative, these infusions will last up to several months in your kitchen or bathroom.

The type of honey you use is important here. Filtered honey is far easier to deal with when infusing since it tends to be thinner and less viscous than raw, unfiltered honey. If your honey is too dense, try gently warming it in a double boiler or microwave before adding the herbs and flowers.

I use honey as my go-to sweetener throughout the book, both because I love its flavor, and because of its exceptional qualities as a preservative, antibacterial agent, and immune system booster.

Honey with Fresh Herbs & Flowers

> **1 part filtered honey (not raw, should be runny)**
>
> **2 parts fresh, clean herbs or flowers**

Remove the fresh herbs or flowers from their stems and leaves, wash, and dry. Fill a small saucepan with 2 inches of water, and nestle a small heatproof bowl over the top to create a double boiler. The water should not touch the bottom. Bring the water to a boil. Add the honey to the bowl, and stir to warm. When the honey is completely liquid and hot to the touch, add the herbs or flowers. Fold in gently and remove from the heat. Let steep for up to 24 hours, then warm to liquid again and strain out the herbs or flowers. Store the honey in an airtight jar.

Honey with Dry Herbs & Flowers

> **2 parts filtered honey**
>
> **1 part dried herb or flower of choice**

Heat the honey per the method above. Place the herbs or flowers in the base of clean, dry jars. Pour the honey on top. Stir to integrate completely. Let cool entirely, then seal. Let steep for up to 24 hours, then warm to liquid again and strain out the herbs or flowers, if desired. Store the honey in an airtight jar.

Infused sugar

Granulated Sugar

Infused sugars can be used in the same way regular sugars can, but will add splashes of subtle flavor to baked goods, frozen treats, beverages, sauces, and puddings. It's important to use entirely dried herbs and flowers here, since any moisture will ruin the sugar.

Unlike oil and honey, sugar takes much longer to infuse—about 2 weeks—unless you make a blended sugar (process also follows).

> **2 parts granulated sugar**
>
> **1 part dried herb or flower of choice**

Mix the sugar and herbs or flowers in an airtight container until evenly distributed. Cover and keep in a cool place for 2 weeks or longer to infuse. For a blended sugar, process the herbs and sugar in a food processor until desired consistency is reached. If you want to leave the herbs or flowers in the sugar, the infusion is ready. If you prefer a sugar sans plant life, strain through a mesh sieve and return to an airtight container.

Simple Syrup

Infused simple syrups are a breeze to make, will last you up to a month, and allow you to add splashes of sweetness and intense flavor to juices, desserts, cocktails, and any other treats you might dream up.

> **1 part granulated sugar**
>
> **1 part water**
>
> **2 parts herb or flower of choice**

Combine the sugar and water in a saucepan and bring to a boil over medium heat, stirring occasionally. Reduce the heat to low, add the herb or flower, and cook for another 1 to 2 minutes. Remove from the heat and let steep at least 30 minutes, then strain and discard the plant material. Store in an airtight container in the fridge, up to 1 month.

Infused salt

Similar to infusing granulated sugar, salts demand moisture-less herbs, so make sure you use hardy fresh herbs (like rosemary and thyme) or dried versions of the herbs and flowers you plan to infuse.

> **2 parts sea salt**
>
> **1 part dried herb or flower of choice**

Mix the salt and the herbs or flowers in an airtight container until evenly distributed. Cover and keep in a cool place for 2 weeks or longer to infuse. For a blended salt, process the herbs and salt in a food processor until desired consistency is reached. If you want to leave the herbs or flowers in the salt, the infusion is ready. If you prefer a salt sans plant life, strain the infused salt through a mesh sieve and return to an airtight container.

HERBS

THE FRAGRANCE AND FLAVOR OF HERBS can be deeply intoxicating, but their healing powers are equally significant. In this section, I'll introduce a few herbal superstars that I use all the time, and that will be invaluable to your kitchen and beauty repertoire.

In the kitchen, my love of herbs is largely rooted in their capacity to transcend traditional savory/sweet classification. With flavors both potent and subtle, herbs can help you to transform the mundane into the extraordinary. Each of the herbs that follows can be used in both savory and sweet capacities.

Preparing herbs to be used as body and beauty products, you'll discover new facets of potency: scents that are capable of transporting the spirit but also of healing the body. Each herb boasts specific curative capacities. Unlocking these secrets will awaken you to a new world of tangible, practical, and completely wholesome self-care.

HERB STORAGE

Herbs fall into two categories: tender herbs and hardy herbs. Tender herbs have pliable leaves and stems with a higher water content—think basil, cilantro, and mint. Hardy herbs have more brittle leaves and stems, and a lower water content—think rosemary, thyme, and oregano.

To store fresh tender herbs, trim their stems like you would a bouquet of flowers, and place them in a glass or jar with at least an inch of water at the bottom. Basil can be kept at room temperature, out of the sun. Other tender herbs should be covered loosely with a plastic bag that goes over the glass, and kept in the fridge.

To store hardy herbs, wash or clean and dry them as necessary, then wrap them in a paper towel and keep them in the fridge in a ziplock bag.

BASIL

FLAVOR PROFILE: Mediterranean, Asian

HERBAL QUALITIES: Joy inspiring, mind soothing, digestion supporting

SAVORY FLAVOR PAIRINGS: Tomatoes, eggplant, feta, olives, olive oil, zucchini, eggs, mozzarella, pasta, corn, garlic, chickpeas, Asian dishes

SWEET FLAVOR PAIRINGS: Strawberries, watermelon, citrus, honey, ice creams and sorbets

CILANTRO

FLAVOR PROFILE: Latin American, Asian

HERBAL QUALITIES: Astringent, digestion supporting, heavy-metal cleansing

SAVORY FLAVOR PAIRINGS: Legumes, Mexican dishes, avocado, lime, rice, peppers, eggplant, soy sauce, yogurt, tomatoes

SWEET FLAVOR PAIRINGS: Citrus, mango, coconut, melons, pineapple

FENNEL

FLAVOR PROFILE: European, Mediterranean, Asian

HERBAL QUALITIES: Digestion supporting, respiratory strengthening, system purifying, estrogenic

SAVORY FLAVOR PAIRINGS: Root vegetables, alliums, citrus, olives, dairy

SWEET FLAVOR PAIRINGS: Apples, pears, citrus, rhubarb

MINT

FLAVOR PROFILE: Mediterranean, Asian

HERBAL QUALITIES: Invigorating, nausea reducing, digestion supporting

SAVORY FLAVOR PAIRINGS: Yogurt, pine nuts, artichokes, lemon, feta, olives, olive oil, soy sauce, chickpeas, Asian dishes

SWEET FLAVOR PAIRINGS: All fruit (favorites include stone fruit, berries, figs, and melons), honey, chocolate, vanilla

OREGANO

FLAVOR PROFILE: Mediterranean, Mexican

HERBAL QUALITIES: Inflammation reducing, antibacterial, respiratory strengthening

SAVORY FLAVOR PAIRINGS: Tomatoes, feta, legumes, citrus

ROSEMARY

FLAVOR PROFILE: European

HERBAL QUALITIES: Respiratory strengthening, memory supporting, system purifying and stimulating

SAVORY FLAVOR PAIRINGS: Nuts, cheeses, root vegetables, winter squash

SWEET FLAVOR PAIRINGS: Citrus, apples, pears, maple, chocolate

SAGE

FLAVOR PROFILE: Mediterranean, European

HERBAL QUALITIES: Respiratory strengthening, sore throat and congestion easing

SAVORY FLAVOR PAIRINGS: Nuts, cheeses, root vegetables, winter squash, alliums

SWEET FLAVOR PAIRINGS: Stone fruit, apples, pears, honey, cranberries, cream

THYME

FLAVOR PROFILE: European

HERBAL QUALITIES: Antiseptic, heartening, respiratory strengthening

SAVORY FLAVOR PAIRINGS: Cheeses, legumes, citrus

SWEET FLAVOR PAIRINGS: Stone fruit, honey, figs, citrus, blackberries

1

BASIL

WHEN NOTHING ELSE WAS GROWING IN OUR GARDEN, there was always basil. Basil was the constant, the perennial survivor, the must-have little black dress of the herbal closet. I remember most vividly basil in the rain, its scent covering my hands in a delicate perfume that urged me to experiment in the kitchen.

I learned to throw basil into just about everything—it sang with olive oil and balsamic on Mediterranean plates as prolifically as it danced with soy sauce and tofu in Asian dishes. The many basil varietals that exist (Thai, purple, cinnamon) serve as a kind of herbal flair: Their leaves beg you to accessorize with abandon, finding unexpected flavor combinations.

Basil has a purity of flavor and scent that can be gentle or strong depending on how you use it. So while it may be most readily reminiscent of nights of pizza, pasta, and formaggio, its healing qualities are equally enticing. In India, certain varietals of basil are called holy and are used to treat internal and external health challenges. Closer to home, your local, garden-variety basil can also be used to treat disturbances of the skin and the digestive system.

nota bene: Basil grows readily almost anywhere, including in city apartment windows and indoor garden boxes. Whether homegrown or harvested from the farmers' market, it remains my trustiest herbal friend.

Discover more of basil's properties on page 20.

Watermelon Cucumber Salad with Crispy Thai Basil Dressing (Vegan)

I do not respond well to heat, fair-skinned redhead that I am. I spent my summers caked in sunscreen, lost in the folds of a damp swim shirt. I was not your typical island child. Though we frequented the beach, our home was in the colder climes of the slopes of Haleakala Crater. The land around my childhood home looks more like Ireland than Hawaii—and I tend to wilt in temperatures higher than 80°F. Come heat, I need water. As much water as possible, in as many forms as possible.

I also find that my digestive system behaves differently when it's hot: I want less food, and I want my food to be cool, cooler, cooling. This salad bridges the gap between the solid and liquid, and celebrates the luscious flavor of Thai basil. Thai basil is similar to regular basil, but it also brings notes of citrus and anise and a gentle spice to the party. It's exquisite.

While savory watermelon dishes are traditionally paired with more Mediterranean flavors, lime highlights Thai basil's Asian roots. Combined with nutty pepitas (pumpkin seeds) and juicy cucumber, these flavors soar.

This is a salad to eat outdoors, in the summer, with sweat dripping down your face. It's a salad to eat when you're not sure if you belong. It's a salad that makes discomfort melt.

serves 2 to 4

preparation time: 18 minutes

CRISPY THAI BASIL DRESSING

¼ cup pepitas (pumpkin seeds), toasted in a dry
   skillet until golden brown

3 tablespoons olive oil

¼ cup fresh Thai basil leaves, thinly sliced

4 pinches sea salt, plus more to taste

1 tablespoon fresh lime juice (about ½ lime)

Pinch of cayenne pepper

WATERMELON CUCUMBER SALAD

5-inch length of Persian cucumber

4 cups watermelon cubes, ½ to 1 inch

MAKE THE DRESSING

Place the oil in a medium frying pan over
medium-high heat. After about 1½ minutes,
test the oil with a droplet of water; if it sizzles,
it's ready. Drop the basil into the oil in a
single layer, and sprinkle with 2 pinches of
salt. Swirl the basil for a count of three, then
remove the pan from the heat and pour the
oil into a heatproof bowl, leaving the crispy
basil in the pan.

   Using a mortar and pestle or the handle
of a knife on a cutting board, gently crush
2 tablespoons of the toasted pepitas. In a
small bowl, combine 2½ tablespoons of the
reserved oil, the lime juice, cayenne, and
the remaining 2 pinches of salt. Whisk to
combine, then stir in the crushed pepitas and
1 tablespoon of the basil. The dressing will
have a consistency similar to pesto. Adjust
salt to taste.

MAKE THE SALAD

Using a vegetable peeler or mandoline, shave
the cucumber into thin slices, either lengthwise or across. Set aside.

   Arrange the watermelon cubes on a
plate in a single layer. Distribute the shaved
cucumber over the watermelon, curling
some pieces between the watermelon cubes.
Spoon the dressing over the watermelon and
cucumber, and finish with the remaining
whole pepitas and basil.

Heirloom Tomato, Feta & Corn Panzanella with Pesto Vinaigrette

I moved to San Francisco two years after my mother died. It was the first move I'd ever made entirely of my own accord, for my own purposes. I'd moved across the country for school, for work, and for men, but never for myself. And never to a real city. I was hungry, deeply hungry, for a life that pulsed outside my own skin. A life that was bigger than the one I knew before.

Among the many gifts of becoming San Francisco gave to me, one of its greatest was the food. The city, in all of its hipster foodie glory, shaped my palate almost as much as my island home had. I learned to feel purpose standing in line for fresh bread at 4:30 p.m. at Tartine, flush with the scent of street jasmine and sidewalk tar, eager for a bread so vital it fed part of the city's soul. I learned to navigate farmers' markets, to get to know the people who grew the plumpest tomatoes, the most biting arugula, the sweetest peas. And I made friends whose palates also changed mine.

The first panzanella I ever had, brought to dinner by my friend Sara, completely rearranged my perception of a salad. Gone were the leafy greens and underdressed veggies, and in their place was a salad as complex as an entire city. There were monuments of crusty bread, rivers of tangy vinaigrette, streets of pickled red onions, souvenirs of toasted sunflower seeds. As far as this was from the traditional panzanella—an Italian salad made from day-old bread, onions, tomatoes, olive oil, vinegar, and seasonings—this infinitely transformable salad had my heart.

This panzanella is a touch closer to the traditional, proffering a tangy pesto vinaigrette with fresh corn, tomatoes, and feta cheese. It's a salad for friends, for change, for redefining what you know.

serves 2 to 3
preparation time: 35 to 45 minutes

PESTO VINAIGRETTE

¼ cup fresh basil leaves, washed and dried

¼ cup olive oil

1 garlic clove, coarsely chopped

2 tablespoons toasted pine nuts

¼ teaspoon sea salt

½ teaspoon white balsamic or other light vinegar (such as red wine vinegar)

Squeeze of fresh lemon juice

PANZANELLA

1½ ears fresh corn (1 to 1½ cups)

2 cups 1- to 2-inch chunks day-old loaf bread of choice

3 medium heirloom tomatoes (any color)

¼ cup crumbled feta cheese (about 1½ ounces, I prefer the feta sold in brine)

Small fresh basil leaves, for garnish

MAKE THE VINAIGRETTE

In a small food processor or blender, combine the basil, oil, garlic, pine nuts, salt, vinegar, and lemon juice. Blend on low or use the pulse function to break down the ingredients until the basil is in small flecks.

MAKE THE PANZANELLA

Preheat the oven to 450°F. Shuck the corn and trim the kernels from the cobs. Set the kernels aside.

Arrange the chunks of bread in a single layer on a rimmed baking sheet. Bake for 2 to 3 minutes, until the bread is toasty and golden brown. Remove from the oven and set aside.

Trim the tops off the tomatoes, then slice them as desired. Some seeds are fine.

Combine the corn, tomatoes, and feta in a large bowl and toss gently. Drizzle with the pesto vinaigrette and add the bread chunks. Toss gently once more, and leave to sit for 15 minutes. Before serving, garnish with basil.

Zucchini Basil Soup with Creamy Hemp Swirl & Garlicky Bread Crumbs (Vegan)

This soup changed my life. I learned the simple blended soup method from a friend on Maui who is a tremendous healer—of spines (she's a chiropractor), of hearts, and of bellies. I'll admit, I was deeply skeptical when Tracey told me we'd be making soup from steamed zucchini. I abhor steamed zucchini, and I couldn't imagine she'd have a miraculous way to change my mind.

But my first taste of the soup she made that day was astonishing. It was vibrant green, with a smooth, rich texture and an earthy taste that was both bright and mellow. There was no zucchini weirdness in sight (or taste). It was filling, packed with vitamins and minerals from the nutritional yeast and hemp seeds, and powerfully vibrant. I felt more alive with every spoonful.

In the years to come, the soup morphed as it became a nourishing staple in my own kitchen. I added herbs I had on hand, and kale and hemp seeds for an extra hit of plant protein. In this version, basil sings a dulcet melody to zucchini, adding a layer of summer sweetness to the soup. The ume plum vinegar (found in the Asian section of most grocery stores) contributes a unique depth, hitting three tastes at once: It is irrepressibly salty, sweet, and sour. The soup is finished with homemade garlicky bread crumbs and topped with a light and creamy hemp swirl that can be blended with olive oil for a delicious salad dressing if you have extra.

serves 4
preparation time: 35 minutes

GARLICKY BREAD CRUMBS

1 cup chunky bread crumbs, from crushed stale bread or torn fresh bread (I love seeded multigrain)

2 tablespoons olive oil

1 garlic clove, finely grated or minced

A few pinches of sea salt

CREAMY HEMP SWIRL

½ cup hemp seeds

½ cup water

1 tablespoon plus 1 teaspoon lemon juice

1 to 2 small garlic cloves, or to taste

½ teaspoon sea salt

ZUCCHINI BASIL SOUP

3½ cups water, for steaming and blending

4 medium zucchini (1½ to 2 pounds), sliced lengthwise and cut into 2-inch pieces

1 medium onion, quartered and layers separated

2 garlic cloves

4 large leaves kale, stems removed and leaves torn

½ teaspoon sea salt

1 tablespoon ume plum vinegar, or 2¼ teaspoons sherry vinegar plus ¾ teaspoon sea salt

2 tablespoons hemp seeds

1 tablespoon olive oil, plus more for drizzling

3 tablespoons nutritional yeast

¾ teaspoon ground coriander

7 large fresh basil leaves, plus more for garnish

Freshly cracked black pepper, to taste

MAKE THE BREAD CRUMBS

Preheat the oven or toaster oven to 450°F. In a small bowl, mix the bread crumbs, oil, garlic, and salt. Toss thoroughly to combine. Place in a single layer on a small baking sheet and bake for 2 to 3 minutes, until just golden brown and fragrant. Remove from the oven and set aside.

MAKE THE HEMP SWIRL

Place the hemp seeds, water, lemon juice, garlic, and salt in a small food processor or blender and process until completely smooth.

MAKE THE SOUP

Fill a large stockpot with the water and bring to a boil, covered, over medium-high heat. Once the water is boiling, place a metal steamer basket in the pot and add the zucchini, onion, and garlic. Replace the lid and steam the vegetables for 8 minutes, then add the kale and steam for 1 more minute, until the zucchini is tender and the onion is just slightly translucent.

Remove from the heat, and transfer the veggies (careful, hot!!!) to a blender. Add 1 to 1½ cups of the steam water (you can add more later if need be, depending how thick you like it). Then add the salt, vinegar, hemp seeds, oil, nutritional yeast, and coriander, and blend on high until everything is fully incorporated. Add the basil and blend until creamy smooth.

Pour the soup into bowls and top with the creamy hemp swirl, bread crumbs, basil, a drizzle of olive oil, and some pepper. Soup is excellent hot or chilled.

Roasted Strawberry & Basil Cream Pie

Going with the flow is not something at which I'm exceptionally skilled, at least when it comes to matters of the heart. While my father moved forward with his life in the wake of my mother's death, finding a new partner, Susan, and making a new world for himself, I clung to my hurt. When he tried to convince me to spend time with him and Susan, I resisted. Susan, patient saint of beauty and composure that she is, knew better than to force the issue. She let me be. She let me feel. She knew it would take time. And she made me cream pie.

The thing is, I'm not a cake person. I've tried to be, I've tried to like its layers and its shapely form. But there's something about cake that just makes me want pie. So when Susan introduced a graham cracker crusted lilikoi (passion fruit) cream cheese pie into my life, I knew I was ready to love her. I decided it was far more delicious to eat lilikoi cream pie than it was to wallow in the bitterness of grief.

Susan's lilikoi cream cheese pie was the inspiration for this whippy, pale pink, basil-infused strawberry version, and I'm not going to lie to you: When I dished this up and my friends took their first bites, someone uttered, "This is what cream pie should be."

This is our first fresh herb infusion, a process I've come to love as much for the poetry of its steps as for the potency of its results. Infusing herbs involves heating a base liquid and then adding the leaves. The heat coaxes out the herb's oils and essence, yielding incredible fragrance and flavor. Infusions do call for a patient hand and a willing heart. The results are always worth it, I promise.

Welcome to the cream pie of my strawberry basil dreams.

serves 6 to 8

preparation time: about 1 hour + 2 hours chill time

BASIL WHIPPED CREAM

1 cup heavy cream

1 cup fresh basil leaves, plus more for garnish

1 tablespoon honey

GRAHAM CRACKER CRUST

6 tablespoons (¾ stick) salted butter

13½ graham crackers (1½ sleeves)

1 tablespoon granulated sugar

¼ teaspoon sea salt

ROASTED STRAWBERRY CREAM FILLING

2 cups strawberries, washed and stemmed, plus 5 to 7 strawberries for garnish

2 tablespoons granulated sugar

1 cup heavy cream

8 ounces cream cheese, at room temperature

⅓ cup honey

MAKE THE WHIPPED CREAM

In a small saucepan, heat the heavy cream over medium heat. When steam rises, slightly crumple the basil leaves, add them to the cream, and reduce the heat to low. Stir and compress the basil with a wooden spoon or silicone spatula, cooking for another 1 to 2 minutes. Do not let the mixture boil. Remove from the heat and let the basil steep for 30 minutes, covered. When the basil has finished steeping, strain the cream and discard the basil.

Let the basil-infused cream cool, then whip with the honey until soft peaks form. Set aside in the fridge.

MAKE THE CRUST

Preheat the oven to 375°F.

In a small saucepan over low heat, melt the butter. Crush the graham crackers in a food processor or blender until they have a sandy texture. Don't over-blend into a flour. Pour the crumbs into a large bowl and mix in the sugar, butter, and salt. Mix until you have a wet sand-like blend.

Press the mixture evenly into the bottom and up the sides of a 9-inch pie pan. Bake for 10 to 12 minutes, until golden brown. Remove and let cool completely on a rack.

MAKE THE FILLING

With the oven still at 375°F, cut the strawberries in half. Place in a large bowl and toss gently with the sugar. Arrange them on a parchment-lined rimmed baking sheet and bake for 25 minutes. Remove from the oven and let cool for 10 minutes. Transfer to a food processor or blender, puree, and set aside to cool completely.

Whip the heavy cream in a large bowl until soft peaks form. Set aside.

In a second bowl, whip the cream cheese, cooled strawberry puree, and honey until completely smooth, about 5 minutes. Fold the whipped cream into the strawberry cream cheese mixture until incorporated and even in color.

ASSEMBLE THE PIE

Once the pie crust is completely cool, spread the strawberry cream cheese mixture into the bottom of the pan. Spoon the basil whipped cream in a smaller circle over the top of the strawberry filling, leaving a 2-inch border.

Garnish with fresh strawberry halves and small basil leaves. Chill, covered in plastic wrap, for at least 2 hours.

Slice and serve with extra strawberries and a sprinkle of minced fresh basil leaves and small, whole leaves for garnish.

Lemongrass Basil Coconut Ice Cream with Black Sesame Brittle

Much like my move to San Francisco, my migration to Los Angeles three years later was an Independent Woman power shift of its own kind. For the first time, I picked out my own apartment, decorated with my own art, found my own furniture, and was in charge of my own kitchen. I'd only ever lived with family, significant others, and roommates, and the transition was monumental. I discovered the joys of peeing with the door open, of running around with no pants on, of having full-force Beyoncé dance marathons any time I damn well pleased.

There was just one small problem. My kitchen was about the size of my bathroom. This is the same kitchen I live with today, and it has stretched my capacity to streamline kitchen work to the farthest reaches of my imagination. It's also limited the number of essential kitchen appliances I keep on hand. And though I never imagined I'd call an ice cream maker essential, when I received one from a friend ready to chuck it, making ice cream quickly became an addiction. It was fun, it was easy, and it was wildly creative.

If you can't stomach the thought of adding this delightful appliance to your kitchen arsenal via purchase new or used, you can make this ice cream without a churning machine. Alternative instructions provided below.

This vegan ice cream melds the buoyant flavors of lemongrass, basil, and coconut with the brightness of lime juice and zest. Finished with earthy black sesame brittle made in minutes from maple syrup and flaky sea salt, it's a savory-sweet dessert as nourishing as it is sophisticated.

makes 1 quart

preparation time: overnight ice cream maker freeze + 40 minutes + 4 to 5 hours chill time

LEMONGRASS BASIL COCONUT ICE CREAM

2 (13.5-ounce) cans coconut milk

1 cup fresh basil leaves

½ cup honey

1½ tablespoons cornstarch

¼ teaspoon sea salt

1½ teaspoons lime zest

2 tablespoons lime juice

6-inch length of fresh lemongrass

1 tablespoon vodka (optional, to keep scoopable)

BLACK SESAME BRITTLE

⅓ cup toasted black sesame seeds

1 tablespoon pure maple syrup

¼ teaspoon lime zest, plus more for garnish

1 generous pinch flaky sea salt

PREPARE YOUR ICE CREAM MAKER

The night before you plan to make the ice cream, freeze the bowl of your ice cream maker.

MAKE THE ICE CREAM

Shake the cans of coconut milk before opening. In a blender, combine the basil with the coconut milk, honey, cornstarch, and salt. Blend until completely smooth, and transfer to a large stockpot. Turn the heat to medium and add 1 teaspoon of the lime zest and 1 tablespoon of the lime juice. Bruise and bend the lemongrass stalk, slightly separating the tubes from each other, and add to the pot. Stir to distribute. Heat over medium heat, stirring, until the mixture thickens enough to coat the back of a spatula. Do not boil.

Remove from the heat, cover, and let the mixture steep 30 minutes to 1 hour, longer for a stronger flavor. Once it has steeped, strain out the lemongrass and stir in the remaining ½ teaspoon lime zest and 1 tablespoon lime juice, and add the vodka, if desired.

Process in the ice cream maker, according to the manufacturer's instructions, until frozen. Pour the frozen ice cream into a freezer-safe pan or dish and freeze for at least 6 hours before eating.

MAKE THE BRITTLE

Preheat the oven (or toaster oven) to 425°F. Place a piece of parchment paper on a small rimmed baking sheet. Combine all the ingredients in a small bowl and mix until the sesame seeds are thoroughly coated. Spread in a thin, even layer on the parchment paper and bake for 5 minutes, checking at 3 minutes to make sure nothing burns. When the brittle is bubbly and fragrant, remove it from the oven and let cool completely. Break into pieces and store in an airtight container.

Serve the ice cream topped with the black sesame brittle and a flourish of extra lime zest.

nota bene: If you don't have an ice cream maker, pour the prepared mixture into a freezer-safe pan or dish, cover, and place in the freezer. After 2 hours, or when the mixture begins to freeze, remove it from the freezer and stir vigorously to break up frozen sections. Repeat every 30 minutes until frozen, another 2 to 3 hours. You can do this using a whisk or spatula, an immersion hand blender, or an electric mixer.

Sparkling Cucumber Basil Lemonade (Vegan)

Though I've been given many gorgeous and deeply generous gifts, one stands out from the others: My Vitamix. A birthday present from an ex-boyfriend the first year we were together, it quickly became one of my most prized possessions. When I made the move from San Francisco to LA with nothing but my packed Prius, the Vitamix was the only kitchen item I brought with me. (And yes, I was consciously attempting to become a Prius-driving, Vitamix-toting caricature of my Californian millennial self.)

The Vitamix became a homing device for my relationship to self-care, as was so much of my relationship with that ex. He cared for me impeccably in the months after my mother died, reading me to sleep each night, holding me through every maelstrom of tears and grief, patiently waiting as I waded through doubt and uncertainty. Even now, though we are no longer together and a shiny new Vitamix has replaced the one he gave me, there is not a day when he and that blender have not been there for me.

And when I'm in the mood for a drink full of whimsy, my blender lets me play endlessly. Enter the sparkling cucumber basil lemonade. It's as refreshing as it is sumptuous, the flavors intensified by using blended fresh ingredients diluted with sparkling water. The first of our herb- and flower-infused tonics, this should be mandatory at every summer picnic.

Like most of the tonics in the book, it transitions seamlessly into cocktail-dom. At the bottom of each recipe, you'll find a *Make it a cocktail!* note, with suggestions for alcohol pairings. Experiment freely and widely.

serves 2

preparation time: 5 minutes

3-inch length of cucumber, chilled and coarsely chopped (about ⅓ cup), plus cucumber slices for garnish

2 to 3 fresh basil leaves, plus more for garnish

¼ cup fresh lemon juice, plus lemon slices for garnish

¼ cup still water

1 tablespoon honey or agave nectar

¾ cup sparkling water, or more to taste

Ice cubes, for serving

Add the chopped cucumber to a blender or food processor with the basil, lemon juice, still water, and honey. Blend until smooth, then distribute evenly between 2 glasses.

Add the sparkling water, again splitting evenly between the glasses. Drop in a few ice cubes, and garnish with cucumber slices, lemon slices, and basil as desired.

MAKE IT A COCKTAIL!
Gin, vodka, light rum, cachaça.

Blackberry Basil Healing Mask

Though I love the flavor of raw honey, I'm far more enamored with its power to soothe and rejuvenate even the most tired and dull skin—and thus begins my official Campaign for Honey as Skincare President™. I've received countless emails from friends and grateful Kale & Caramel readers whose skin completely transformed after they started using honey as face wash. This healing mask takes the soothing quotient to the next level with freshly crushed basil leaves and juicy blackberries.

Basil, in its many forms, has long been revered for its healing properties in India, where it's known to soothe everything from digestion to inflammation. This mask applies fresh basil leaves directly to the skin, allowing the herb to work its magic alongside the antibacterial, anti-aging powers of raw honey. Blackberries join the party to tone the skin with gentle fruit acids and vitamin C.

Together, these three ingredients form the foundation of a skin treatment that proves you need look no further than your fridge to get your glow on.

makes about ¼ cup
preparation time: 5 minutes

5 blackberries or other fresh berries
3 tablespoons raw, unfiltered honey

5 fresh basil leaves, minced

In a small bowl, crush the blackberries and strain out the juice into a second bowl. Add the honey and basil to the blackberry juice and stir to combine, using pressure to crush the basil into the honey. When fully incorporated, spread 1½ teaspoons onto clean skin and let sit for 5 to 10 minutes. Then wash off completely and follow with toning spritz and Jasmine Facial Oil (page 204).

Store the remainder in an airtight container in the fridge for up to 1 week.

2

CILANTRO

REAL TALK: I DIDN'T EAT CILANTRO for the first twenty years of my life. Then, in an extraordinary turn of palatal events, my tastes changed, and the flavor of cilantro was no longer nauseating to me. Its sharp notes are now exciting where they were once threatening.

Cilantro is a grown-up flavor, imparting a rigorous, sharp dimension of taste that is at once unexpected and necessary. Once you discover the edge that cilantro lends to a perfect guacamole or a steaming bowl of Vietnamese phở, it's hard to go back. Cilantro is a sexy lover of an herb—not for everyone every day, but impossible to forget.

The herb also won me over in its role as a heavy-metal cleanser and medicinal superfood. When my mom was sick and attempting to slow the steady march of her disease, she looked to eliminate toxins through nutritional cleansing. Cilantro, in significant quantities, is considered an excellent agent to remove heavy metals from the body. These toxins may otherwise accumulate in the blood and brain, straining the immune system and damaging neuronal processes.

Though the recipes here may not contain medicinal levels of cilantro, the herb's cleansing essence is present in every bite, every sip.

Discover more of cilantro's properties on page 20.

Black Bean Bisque with Cilantro Lime Crema

I spent most of the first two and a half decades of my life reaching out to a future self I was sure was already inside me, if only I would act older and wiser and far more serious than I was. At nineteen, I spent hours each day meditating. At twenty-one, I memorized Sanskrit texts from ancient tomes, and soon I stopped reading fiction, stopped watching TV, stopped listening to pop music. And then, when I was twenty-four, my mother died.

Almost instantaneously, my longing for adulthood ceased. In the wake of her death and the space carved out by grief, I suddenly wanted to be exactly what and who I was. I didn't want to be older. If anything, I wanted to be much, much younger. I felt exposed. Supremely childlike. Things I thought were one way were actually another. What was up was down. I no longer had any answers.

Soon, I began to relish the not knowing. I relaxed in the open palm of seeing and experiencing rather than longing for or grasping after. I blasted Christina Aguilera and Beyoncé. I binge-watched *Gossip Girl*. I let myself be.

This dish is my favorite comfort food (a bowl of black beans) soupified and wilded up with cilantro lime crema. It's smoky, it's sultry, and gosh darn it, it's totally sexy. Let these beans seduce you with their tangy lime, their spicy chipotle and jalapeño, and, yes, their beaniness. Let the waves of cilantro wash over you, just exactly as you are.

serves 3 to 4
preparation time: about 45 minutes

BLACK BEAN BISQUE

2 tablespoons olive oil

1 medium yellow onion, thinly sliced

2 garlic cloves, coarsely chopped

½ jalapeño pepper, seeded and coarsely chopped

½ teaspoon ground chipotle pepper

¼ teaspoon ground paprika

¼ teaspoon ground coriander

2 (15-ounce) cans black beans (about 3 cups)

2 tablespoons fresh cilantro leaves

¾ teaspoon sea salt

1 tablespoon plus 1 teaspoon lime juice

1½ cups vegetable broth

¼ teaspoon cayenne pepper, for more heat (optional)

Hot sauce, for garnish (optional)

CILANTRO LIME CREMA

¼ medium avocado, plus remaining avocado for garnish

1 teaspoon lime juice

2 pinches sea salt

¼ cup sour cream, plus more for garnish

1 tablespoon minced fresh cilantro, plus whole leaves for garnish

MAKE THE BISQUE

Place the oil, onion, garlic, and jalapeño in a large stockpot over medium heat. Add the chipotle, paprika, and coriander. Stir with a wooden spoon or spatula to incorporate, and sauté for 20 to 25 minutes, until the onion is translucent.

Add the beans, cilantro, salt, and the 1 tablespoon lime juice. Stir to incorporate, and bring to a simmer. Reduce the heat and let simmer, covered, for 7 to 10 minutes, until fragrant. Remove from the heat.

Transfer three-fourths of this mixture to a blender, add the vegetable broth, and blend until smooth. Return the blended soup to

the pot, mix with the remaining soup base, and add the 1 teaspoon lime juice. Stir to incorporate. Taste, and stir in the cayenne for extra spice, if desired.

MAKE THE CREMA

In a medium bowl, use a fork to mash the avocado with the lime juice and salt. Once the mixture is creamy, blend in the sour cream and cilantro.

Serve the soup topped with the cilantro lime crema and garnish with avocado, sour cream, and cilantro. Drizzle with hot sauce, if desired.

Black Sesame-Crusted Tofu Bowl Bar with Quick Pickled Veggies & Cilantro Tahini Sauce (Vegan)

When I was a teenager, I bought my mom one of those fridge magnets with the illustrations of 1950s housewives standing gleefully over their stoves, except this one said, "What *couldn't* that woman do with tofu!" It fit perfectly: She truly was a tofu queen.

We lived in a small house that was riddled with termites but full of love and arguments and excellent tofu. My dad would often coax my mom to dance with him on the small bit of wood flooring in the open kitchen, the two of them in their inside-only Birkenstocks and their socks. My dad's soft, practical hands and my mom's long fingers, their deep brown eyes laughing at each other, the two of them dancing. To Sinatra. Swaying to, "Our love is here to stay."

Sometimes I felt embarrassed watching them in what seemed like such a private moment, their romance, their singing to each other, my dad in his hopeful croon promising his love to my mom, my mom utterly surrendered to everything they were together, all the ways their love had stayed. Had lasted. Even as the house around them crumbled. Even as her body crumbled.

She knew how to cook tofu, and so would I.

This black sesame-studded tofu is a riff on the baked ginger tofu she'd make at least once a week when I was younger. By now you're probably on to another favorite of mine: sesame. Tahini was a childhood staple, drizzled on sprouted-wheat bagels, rice cakes, fresh fruit, and steamed veggies (aka Hippie Cuisine 101, thankyouverymuch). Which brings me to this luscious sesame-crusted tofu with cilantro tahini sauce.

Speaking of sauce, let's get our hands sticky with miso for the first (but definitely not last) time in the book. Miso is a fermented paste made from legumes or grains, rich in umami, and full of digestion-supporting probiotic cultures. Using miso paste is an easy way to boost flavor in vegan dishes, and, when mixed with flavors like tahini and cilantro, miso becomes a kind of universal solvent—it seamlessly softens their bitterness with tang and sweetness.

This is the perfect meal to make for a dinner party or a family dinner: It comes together quickly, it's infinitely customizable, and it's super delish.

serves 4

preparation time: 40 minutes

BASMATI RICE

1 cup white basmati rice

2 cups water

BLACK SESAME-CRUSTED TOFU

1 block (about 14 ounces) firm tofu

4 tablespoons soy sauce

1 teaspoon ume plum vinegar or rice vinegar

2 teaspoons grated fresh ginger

1 tablespoon toasted sesame oil

1 tablespoon olive oil

3 tablespoons black or white sesame seeds

CUCUMBER LIME SALAD

1 tablespoon fresh lime juice

¾ cup thinly sliced cucumber

1 teaspoon minced fresh cilantro, plus cilantro leaves for garnish

A few pinches of sea salt, or to taste

QUICK PICKLED VEGGIES

2 medium carrots, washed and tops trimmed, thinly julienned (about ¾ cup)

⅓ medium watermelon radish (or radish of choice), washed, trimmed, and thinly sliced

1 tablespoon ume plum vinegar, or 2¼ teaspoons sherry vinegar plus ¾ teaspoon sea salt

1 tablespoon plus 1 teaspoon apple cider vinegar

1 tablespoon water

1 tablespoon fresh mint leaves, minced

CILANTRO TAHINI SAUCE

¼ cup tahini

1 teaspoon ume plum vinegar, or ¾ teaspoon sherry vinegar plus ¼ teaspoon sea salt

1 teaspoon miso paste

5 tablespoons water

1 small garlic clove, crushed

1 tablespoon loosely packed fresh cilantro leaves

GARNISH

1 sheet toasted nori seaweed, cut into small pieces

½ avocado, sliced

MAKE THE RICE

Place the rice and water in a medium saucepan, cover, and bring to a boil (about 5 minutes). Once it boils, reduce the heat to the lowest setting possible and cook for another 20 to 25 minutes, covered, until the water has evaporated and the rice is fluffy. Remove from the heat and set aside.

MAKE THE TOFU

Preheat the oven to 400°F. Line a large rimmed baking sheet with parchment paper. Drain the tofu and cut it into 2-inch-long by ½-inch-thick slabs. Lay the tofu evenly on the baking sheet, with ½ inch between each piece.

In a small bowl, mix the soy sauce, ume plum vinegar, ginger, sesame oil, and olive oil until well combined. Pour over the tofu, coating evenly so that the bottom of each piece also gets some marinade. Sprinkle with the sesame seeds, allowing them to cover both the top and the sides of each piece of tofu.

Bake for 20 to 25 minutes, checking at 15 minutes to assess the level of crispy brownness. Remove when the desired crispiness has been reached!

MAKE THE SALAD

Mix the lime juice, cucumber, cilantro, and salt in a small bowl. Let sit until ready to serve.

MAKE THE PICKLED VEGGIES

Combine the carrots and radish with the vinegars, water, and mint, and toss to mix thoroughly. Continue to toss until the carrots and radish soften slightly. Let sit until ready to serve.

MAKE THE SAUCE

Combine the tahini, ume plum vinegar, miso paste, water, and garlic in a small food processor or blender and blend on high to combine. Once fully homogenized, add the cilantro and pulse to chop the cilantro into small flecks. Pour into a bowl or sauce vessel and set aside.

ASSEMBLE THE BOWL BAR

Place the nori, avocado, extra cilantro, cilantro tahini sauce, quick pickles, cucumber lime salad, tofu, and rice on the dining table with bowls and serving utensils and let everyone create their own work of bowl food art.

Coconut Ginger Tapioca with Cilantro-Scented Mango (Vegan)

On Maui, the days were long and slow, filled with salt air and sunshine. After homework was done, we'd pick up sushi rolls and coconut tapioca and this weird thing called kombucha (it was the '90s—nobody drank kombucha then) on the way to the beach and picnic under the iron-woods with the salt from crashing waves infusing every bite. Sometimes there would be fresh mango, picked in the drylands of Kihei or Lahaina, hot from the sun and dripping with a deep orange juice.

These days taught me how to be still, to listen, to understand that there would always be a force much greater than my own mind—that nature and wind and wave were the constants. That everything tasted better by the ocean.

This is a dessert for the days when I can't get to the ocean, when I am far from home, when I have a million things to do and lazy afternoons in the sand are nowhere on the horizon. It's a dessert for comfort and ease and psycho-spiritual transfusions of sunshine. For mango tinged with lime and mellowed by the bright pop of cilantro.

For breath to come easy, like the ocean.

serves 4 to 6

preparation time: 20 minutes + 4 or more hours chill time

COCONUT GINGER TAPIOCA

1½ cups full-fat coconut milk

1¼ cups unsweetened almond milk

¼ cup water

⅓ cup small tapioca pearls (not instant tapioca)

¼ cup honey or agave

1 teaspoon finely grated fresh ginger (using a Microplane zester or box grater), or minced ginger

¼ teaspoon vanilla seeds scraped from the pod, or ½ teaspoon pure vanilla extract

¼ teaspoon sea salt

CILANTRO-SCENTED MANGO

¾ cup chopped mango

1 teaspoon lime juice

1 teaspoon agave nectar

1 tablespoon coarsely chopped fresh cilantro leaves

Sea salt, to taste

Bee pollen, for garnish

MAKE THE TAPIOCA

At least 2 hours, and up to 24 hours, before you intend to make the tapioca, place the coconut milk, almond milk, and water in a saucepan over low heat for just a few seconds to melt any coconut milk solids. Remove from the heat and stir in the tapioca pearls. Let sit, covered, for at least 2 hours to soften the tapioca.

Once the tapioca has soaked, place the pan over medium heat and add the honey, ginger, vanilla, and salt, and bring to a boil, stirring constantly. Reduce the heat to low and continue stirring while the pudding begins to thicken. After about 10 minutes, or when the tapioca beads are clear and tender to bite, remove from the heat and chill in a covered container in the refrigerator before serving. The pudding will thicken completely once it is chilled.

MAKE THE MANGO

When ready to serve, gently toss the mango in a small bowl with the lime juice, agave, cilantro, and salt. Top the chilled pudding with the cilantro-scented mango and bee pollen.

Green Ice Cream

Here's where I confess that I really, profoundly enjoy weird food. I like food that's arresting, bracing, healing, magical. I like food that shakes up my perception of what it should be. Which is why, one spring day in 2015, I fell in love with Jeni's Garance Vert Clair ice cream—one of a line of ice creams inspired by the distinct hues used by painter Henri Matisse. Aesthete and food lover that I am, I was obsessed. I sampled each one slowly, dutifully, seeing if I could experience each flavor as a synesthetic whole of color and taste, rather than as flavor alone.

The green in particular stole my heart. It was the shimmering teal of the taffeta dress I wore when I played Mother Earth in our fifth grade Waldorf school play about composting. It was the color of my teenage dreams, haunted by mossy pre-Raphaelite visions. It was just one shade lighter than the deep green nail polish Gwyneth Paltrow wore in *Great Expectations* when she and Ethan Hawke had their epic kiss in the rain. And when I met Jeni Britton Bauer (of Jeni's Splendid Ice Creams) in person last spring and she confessed to me her background in scent and perfume, I understood why I'd been so immediately captivated.

Conducting research to make my own version, I learned they'd used spirulina (a chlorophyll- and protein-dense blue-green algae superfood grown in Hawaii—be still my heart) for color, and lemongrass and cilantro for flavor. At home, I decided to add kaffir lime, whose perfume and tang contribute a whole new layer of synesthetic impression. The color was deeply healing. The taste was transportive—a grassy, honey-laden meadow of herbs.

Finished with bee pollen sprinkles, green ice cream is both the perfect way to load up on superfoods in dessert form and, quite simply, a whole lot of fun.

makes about 1 quart
preparation time: overnight ice cream maker
freeze + 40 minutes + 6 to 7 hours chill time

2½ cups whole milk

1½ cups heavy cream

½ cup honey

¼ teaspoon sea salt

10-inch piece of fresh lemongrass

¾ cup fresh cilantro leaves

6 kaffir lime leaves (optional)

2 egg yolks

1½ teaspoons spirulina powder

Bee pollen, for garnish

PREPARE YOUR ICE CREAM MAKER

The night before you plan to make the ice cream, freeze the bowl of your ice cream maker.

MAKE THE ICE CREAM

Heat the milk, heavy cream, honey, and salt in a large saucepan over medium-high heat, stirring frequently. Break the lemongrass into 3-inch pieces and bruise and unravel the stalks to release their flavor. Similarly, slightly crumple the cilantro and the kaffir lime leaves, if using, just to release their oils. Add the herbs to the milk mixture.

Bring to a boil, then remove from the heat. Let sit for 2 hours to infuse the flavor.

When the milk has steeped as long as you'd like it to, pour it through a strainer back into the saucepan, discarding the herbs. Thoroughly whisk in the egg yolks and turn the heat to medium-low. Continue to cook, whisking constantly, until the custard reaches 170°F, 20 to 25 minutes—or until it thickens slightly and coats the back of a spoon. Remove from the heat and pour into a heatproof bowl. Chill in an ice bath or the fridge until completely cool.

Once the custard is cool, whisk in the spirulina powder, making sure to eliminate all clumps as you go.

Assemble and turn on the ice cream maker. Freeze the custard in the ice cream maker, according to the manufacturer's instructions, then transfer to a freezer-safe dish and cover with plastic wrap or a lid. Freeze for at least 4 hours prior to serving. Eat in waffle cones with bee pollen sprinkles!

No ice cream maker? The results won't be as refined, but follow the process on page 38.

Pineapple Cilantro Cleanser (Vegan)

I need to tell you something. Come closer, so I can whisper it. Promise you won't tell? *I've never had a mai tai.* I know, I know. I'm from Hawaii! How is it even possible? The truth is, pineapple juice just never seemed very sexy to me. Until, that is, it met its match in lime and cilantro and the kick of cayenne pepper. Suddenly I got very interested, particularly as I began to learn about cilantro's superhero herbal powers.

Cilantro is considered to be an excellent cleanser of heavy metals (such as lead and mercury) and toxic compounds (such as plastics) that infiltrate our systems through our environment—the air we breathe, the food we eat, the water we drink, the cars we drive, and the products we put on our bodies. Detoxing from heavy metals is a process called chelation, and some research has shown that cilantro has positive effects in supporting this process.

I'm no scientist, but I'll take any extra heavy-metal cleansing I can get, beginning with this super-delish pineapple cilantro cleanser. This frothy, sour-sweet blend will do over a mai tai any day of the week.

serves 2

preparation time: 5 minutes

3 cups chilled fresh or frozen pineapple cubes

½ cup water

2 tablespoons lime juice

3 drops stevia, or sweetener of choice

4 ice cubes

Pinch of sea salt

1 tablespoon fresh cilantro leaves, plus more
   for garnish

Cayenne pepper, for garnish

Place the pineapple, water, lime juice, stevia, ice, and salt in a high-speed blender and blend until completely smooth. Add the cilantro and blend on low until the cilantro leaves are large flecks. Serve immediately, garnished with cayenne and extra cilantro.

MAKE IT A COCKTAIL!
Add tequila, mezcal, vodka, or rum for a—ahem—different kind of cleanse.

3

FENNEL

WE COULDN'T STOP LAUGHING. We laughed until the chic Italians craned their heads to see who the noisy Americans were that were causing all the ruckus. And even then, we couldn't stop. The truth was, we didn't know why. We knew only that we were exhausted, drained of angst by traveling halfway around the globe, giddy with the deliciousness of creamy braised fennel, pesto, fresh gnocchi, and the scent of wisteria.

It was spring in Italy. Archways dripping with purple buds. Before death took her from us, when being was simply laughing and ease, not weighted with the memory of where she said what, and how, and with whom. Not burdened with longing. It was my first taste of fennel. The night I wore my first perfume.

It wasn't until that balmy evening in my fifteenth year of life, in Florence with my parents, that I learned how delicious fennel could be under high heat. Later, an adult in California, I learned to eat it shaved, in salads, roasted, and juiced. Working with the culinary magician Amanda Chantal Bacon, I discovered fennel's medicinal properties, its ability to soothe hormones, and its function as a phytoestrogenic plant.

What makes fennel such a legend to me, though, is the ability to use every part of the plant. The dense root can be roasted, sautéed, caramelized, juiced, or eaten raw, the stalk can be crunched on in salads or any way you might eat celery, and the frond makes a fragrant contribution to soups and garnishes. Finally, dried fennel seeds provide exquisite bursts of flavor in roasted veggies, breads, and soups, effortlessly straddling the line between Asian spices and Mediterranean flavors.

As versatile and sensually evocative as fennel may be in the kitchen, to me it will always be a spring evening in Fiesole, a moment when my parents and I were happy, and whole, and totally free.

Discover more of fennel's properties on page 20.

Blood Orange & Fennel Salad with Oil-Cured Olives (Vegan)

The first time I made this salad I ate the entire three or four servings of it directly off the plate with my hands. It's a salad for summer as much as winter, as its bright flavors lend themselves just as easily to sunshine and heat as they do to the chill of peak citrus season. I also love it because it's a bit of a sleeper: It could easily be self-conscious of its simplicity, its lack of showiness, its six ingredients—including salt and pepper.

But while its ingredients may be simple, together they create an alchemy of flavor that is perfect. It lacks nothing: Salty, sweet, bitter, sour, and spicy flavors are all present. If you have yet to try oil-cured olives, now is your moment. They're meatier than typical olives, and slightly more bitter. They lend what would otherwise be an exceptionally light and bright salad a becoming degree of gravitas.

Fennel here is at its most perfect, in a truly raw state. You can taste every nuance of the herb, and shaving it and pairing it with the acid of blood orange and olive renders it tender without heat. A light dusting of fennel frond adds dimensionality to the fennel flavor, and a welcome burst of green.

serves 4

preparation time: 15 to 20 minutes

3 medium blood oranges or regular oranges

½ medium fennel bulb, fronds separated and reserved

¼ cup oil-cured (or Kalamata) olives, pitted and quartered

2 to 3 tablespoons olive oil

Flaky sea salt, to taste

Freshly cracked black pepper, to taste

Trim the top and bottom of each orange, and stand it up on a cutting board. Now trim the skin from the flesh, cutting downward along the curve of the orange. Cut out each section of fruit, leaving only the membranes, and set the orange segments on a plate. In thicker orange segments, make a long cut to slice the segment in half, making it into 2 slices.

Wash and remove the bruised outer layers of the fennel bulb. Slice in half, top down, and then slice the fennel as thinly as possible using a knife, food processor, or mandoline.

Layer the orange and fennel slices on a platter in a concentric circle, or toss together in a bowl if you prefer. Add the olives and the fennel fronds, and drizzle with the oil. Top with a sprinkle of salt and pepper.

Lemony Fennel, Radish & Kale Salad

I receive one twinkly-eyed question nearly without fail whenever I share the name of my website: *Do you eat kale and caramel together?* I'm left to confess that not only do I never combine the two, I've never even wanted to try. The name for the blog came to me one night, mid-dishwashing, as my friend and mentor Rebecca was urging me to create a digital home for my food and writing. *But what would I call it?* I lamented. I summoned to mind the two foods I could think of that I loved most: Kale. And caramel. And thus the blog was born. At the risk of sounding too heady, it was more a concept than a suggestion for a new flavor combination.

In the hours after I'd logged on to tumblr and registered kaleandcaramel.tumblr.com as legitimate online real estate, I realized that the vibrant health of kale and the sumptuous, playful deliciousness of caramel were two tenets of how I lived my life. Many a kale salad later, Kale & Caramel had become my full-time job, my baby, my exotically named sanctuary on the Internet.

Which brings us to this kale salad, a paean to all things spring, to the powerful fusion of fresh vegetables and herbs and lemon and feta, to the brightness of unadulterated flavors in symphony with each other. There is no kitchen wizardry here, simply a sweet union of diverse textures shot through with the tenderness of olive oil–massaged kale. Yes, massaged. It's kale (and caramel) all grown up.

serves 4 to 6
preparation time: 25 minutes

8 large leaves dinosaur (lacinato) kale

1 tablespoon extra-virgin olive oil

2 cups sugar snap peas, washed and ends trimmed

3 cups very thinly sliced or shaved fennel bulb (about 1 medium-large), fronds reserved

5 to 6 radishes, very thinly sliced or shaved, about 1 cup

⅓ cup loosely packed fresh flat-leaf parsley leaves

⅓ cup loosely packed fresh mint leaves

1 to 2 tablespoons fresh lemon juice, or to taste

A few pinches of flaky sea salt, or to taste

⅓ cup crumbled feta cheese (about 1¾ ounces; I prefer the feta sold in brine)

Freshly cracked black pepper, to taste

Remove the stems from the kale and chop the leaves into thin strips. Place the strips of kale in a large bowl and massage with the oil, about 30 seconds, until the leaves grow deep green, reduce in volume, and take on a mellow sheen.

Slice each sugar snap pea in half diagonally across its midsection to reveal some of the peas. Add the sliced peas, fennel, and radishes to the bowl with the massaged kale.

On a cutting board, give the parsley, mint leaves, and the reserved fennel fronds a coarse chop. Add to the bowl of kale and veggies. Add 1 tablespoon of the lemon juice and the salt, and toss vigorously to combine. Add the feta and toss gently to integrate. Taste and adjust the salt and lemon juice as desired. Finish with freshly cracked pepper, as desired.

Serve immediately. The salad will keep in an airtight container in the fridge for up to 3 days.

Roasted Root Veggies with Fennel & Pistachio Yogurt

I cannot stand cooked carrots. For most of my life, I found absolutely nothing redeeming about them whatsoever. Their texture was appalling, their flavor at once astringent and cloying. I could say, without hesitation, that I'd never met a cooked carrot I liked. And then I discovered my favorite restaurant in California, a place that did things with vegetables that could be described as nothing other than sexy. More specifically, they roasted carrots and served them with ingredients like fennel pollen and yogurt.

Suddenly, I was overwhelmed with the realization that I might, in fact, enjoy cooked carrots. But why? What had changed? Aside from the magical introduction of fennel, a little something called the Maillard reaction, or caramelizing, had occurred. Caramelization is an interaction between sugars and amino acids that occurs during browning—and a flavor profile I gravitated toward before I knew caramelizing veggies was a hip thing to do. It was simply the only way I liked my carrots hot.

While stovetop caramelizing is a fun, hands-on way to get my Maillard on, oven roasting is a totally hands-off method that offers the same results, sometimes faster. This dish caramelizes fennel, shallots, carrots, beets, and sweet potatoes, and tops it all off with cooling yogurt, fennel fronds, and the crunch of pistachio.

serves 4
preparation time: 50 to 60 minutes

ROASTED ROOT VEGGIES

1 tablespoon plus 1 teaspoon whole fennel seeds

½ teaspoon whole cumin seeds

1 medium fennel bulb, washed and trimmed, fronds reserved

4 to 5 carrots, washed and trimmed

2 small-medium beets, washed and trimmed

1 medium sweet potato, washed

¾ cup thinly sliced shallots

¼ cup olive oil

½ teaspoon ground cumin

1 teaspoon flaky sea salt

FENNEL AND PISTACHIO YOGURT

⅓ cup shelled roasted pistachios

⅔ cup yogurt

1 tablespoon olive oil

Flaky sea salt, to taste

MAKE THE VEGGIES

Preheat the oven to 450°F. Line a large rimmed baking sheet with parchment paper.

Crush the whole fennel and cumin seeds with a mortar and pestle until just slightly broken.

Cut the fennel bulb in half, and then into ¼-inch-thick slices. Slice the carrots into long juliennes, about ½ inch thick. Slice the beets into quarters or sixths. Slice the sweet potato into midsize wedges that are roughly the same thickness as the beets.

Place the fennel, carrots, beets, sweet potato, and shallots on the baking sheet in a single layer, mixing to distribute evenly. Drizzle with the oil, and sprinkle with the crushed fennel and cumin seeds, ground cumin, and salt. Toss to coat evenly. Roast for 40 minutes, rotating the pan and turning over the veggies with a spatula halfway through.

MAKE THE YOGURT

Coarsely chop the pistachios and the reserved fennel fronds. Combine the yogurt, oil, 2 teaspoons of the fennel fronds, and a few sprinkles of salt in a small bowl. Top with some of the chopped pistachios and the remaining fennel fronds, reserving some for the veggies.

Serve the roasted veggies with the yogurt, sprinkled with extra pistachios and fennel fronds.

Caramelized Fennel, Chèvre & Kabocha Galette

Coming from Maui, my first experience of seasons as a freshman at Yale felt nothing short of miraculous. I'd never seen such a celebration of color, never felt the changing weather churn inside of me, turning my body into the soft animal thing that it is, never smelled leaves falling into the gentle decay of autumn. Even the light was different. I felt like I could breathe.

I discovered that I loved—craved—autumn because it came as a cooling shroud over the blinding exposure of summertime. Heat, light, intensity, and noise receded into the quieter arms of fall. The coolness, the opportunity for warmth in flavor, was a reprieve, a moment to catch my breath, a moment to remember. Before one year became the next, a few months to reflect, to rebuild the wild.

Fall is also the perfect time for our first galette. I started making galettes because pies always felt a bit prim and proper for my island-girl forager-meets-foodie taste. A galette, though, was a kitchen companion I could seriously get down with. Galettes are free-form pastries adaptable to any flavor palate, they accept the produce of every season, they flex sweet and savory, and—most important—they're effortlessly elegant.

The flavors of fall are, too, a relief for me. Here, the galette's elegance draws upon the tastes of autumn: fleshy orange kabocha squash, wild mushrooms, and caramelized fennel and onion.

nota bene: Always grate the butter for your pastry. Yes, using a cheese grater. Yes, it will change your life into a flaky, buttery dream. Yes, you're welcome.

serves 6 to 8

preparation time: about 1 hour 40 minutes

FENNEL PASTRY CRUST

1¾ cups plus 2 tablespoons all-purpose flour

¾ teaspoon sea salt

¾ teaspoon granulated sugar

1½ tablespoons fresh fennel fronds (from the fennel bulb below), coarsely chopped

6 ounces (1½ sticks) salted butter, chilled

3 to 4 tablespoons ice water, or as needed to bring the dough together

FILLING

1 pound kabocha squash or any winter squash, peeled, seeded, and sliced ¼ inch thick

1 tablespoon olive oil

½ teaspoon sea salt, plus more to sprinkle

CARAMELIZED FENNEL AND ONION

2 cups thinly sliced yellow onion

1 cup thinly sliced fennel bulb

3 tablespoons olive oil

2 tablespoons balsamic vinegar

½ teaspoon sea salt

WILD MUSHROOMS

8 medium to large fresh oyster or chanterelle mushrooms, sliced (about 1½ cups)

2 teaspoons fresh rosemary leaves, plus more for garnish

GALETTE TOPPINGS

1¾ ounces crumbled chèvre (goat cheese, about ⅓ cup)

Flaky sea salt

1 egg (for the egg wash)

MAKE THE CRUST

In a large bowl, whisk the flour, salt, sugar, and fennel fronds. Grate the butter into the dry mixture using a cheese grater. Add the ice water 1 tablespoon at a time, using your hands to incorporate the butter and flour into a ball of dough that is smooth and just sticks together. Flatten the dough into a ½-inch disk, cover with plastic wrap, and place in the fridge while you prep the filling.

MAKE THE FILLING

Preheat the oven to 425°F. Line a baking sheet with parchment paper. Place the squash in a single layer on the baking sheet and drizzle with the 1 tablespoon oil, sprinkle with salt, and toss to combine. Roast for 15 to 20 minutes, checking at 10 minutes for tenderness. The squash should be tender when pierced with a fork, but it doesn't need to be browning (it's going in for a second round with the galette). Remove from the oven and set aside, but leave the oven on.

MAKE THE FENNEL AND ONION

Place the onion, fennel, the 3 tablespoons oil, the vinegar, and ½ teaspoon salt in a large frying pan. Sauté on medium heat, stirring occasionally, until the vegetables are deep brown, with some caramelization around the edges, and have reduced significantly in volume, 20 to 25 minutes. Transfer the fennel and onion to a bowl, leaving the oil and juicy goodness in the pan.

MAKE THE MUSHROOMS

Place the sliced mushrooms and rosemary in the same pan you used for the fennel and onion. Turn the heat to low, and toss them in the oil left in the pan. Sauté gently, 5 to 7 minutes, until most of the liquid released has evaporated and the mushrooms are tender. Remove from the heat.

ASSEMBLE THE GALETTE

Reduce the oven temperature to 400°F. When the dough has chilled for at least 30 minutes, remove it from the fridge and dust a piece of parchment paper with flour (the dough will stay on this parchment paper for baking, so it can be as big as the baking sheet you'll bake on). With a lightly floured rolling pin, roll the dough into a larger circle until it reaches ¼ inch thickness. Place the parchment paper and dough on a large rimmed baking sheet.

Spread the fennel and onion mixture evenly over the center of dough, leaving a 2- to 3-inch perimeter of dough to fold over. Arrange the squash in concentric circles, from outside in, atop the fennel and onion. Top with the mushrooms, cheese, an extra sprinkle of rosemary, and flaky sea salt.

Fold the edges of the galette in and over, making sure to seal it up as you go—no cracks allowed!

In a small bowl, lightly beat the egg. Brush the exposed dough with the egg wash.

Bake for 40 to 45 minutes, until the dough is golden brown.

Fennel Butternut Miso Soup with Toasted Seeds (Vegan)

This recipe was one that was truly born of abandon, of tiredness leading to rifling through leftovers and a raucous throwing of ingredients into a pot. I'd been sick all week while my friend Lindsay and I were on vacation in Maui, just days after Thanksgiving. We spent the afternoon at the beach, lying on the sand in the shelter of a lava-rock cliff, alternating dips in the ocean with long stretches of air-drying until salt formed small crusted ridges in the smalls of our backs.

Two single women in our thirties, both artists, both motherless, both woefully hopeful, we discussed the men in our lives. The men we wanted. The husbands we knew would come, one day.

And then, in the deepening afterglow of sunset, we drove home and mostly what we wanted was soup. Warmth for the cool mountain air that held a sky so full of stars it was a perennial reminder that there was something much bigger than us and our longing. I had fennel left over from making a galette (that precedes this recipe) for Thanksgiving, and I rummaged through the fridge to find other earthy, warming flavors. Miso. Sesame. Butternut. And a uniting bridge of coconut milk, drawing all the flavors together.

The soup is topped with a toasted seed mix, tangy cream of choice, and some minced fennel for texture. It's a party in your mouth, a soup for warmth and friendship and hope.

serves 3 to 4
preparation time: 25 to 30 minutes

FENNEL BUTTERNUT MISO SOUP

3 cups roasted or steamed butternut squash
  (canned is also fine)

1 medium onion, sliced

1 medium fennel bulb, washed and sliced, plus
  ¼ cup minced fennel fronds for garnish

¼ cup olive oil

¼ teaspoon sea salt

¼ teaspoon cayenne pepper, plus more for
  garnish

½ teaspoon ground coriander

1 (13.5-ounce) can full-fat coconut milk

1 cup vegetable broth

¼ cup plus 2 tablespoons miso paste

TOASTED SEEDS

1 teaspoon raw virgin coconut oil

2 tablespoons raw sesame seeds

1 tablespoon fennel seeds, lightly crushed with a
  mortar and pestle or spice grinder

Flaky sea salt

Coconut milk or plain yogurt, for drizzling

MAKE THE SOUP

Puree the squash in a food processor or blender until completely smooth. Set aside.

Place the onion and sliced fennel in a stockpot or large saucepan with the oil, salt, cayenne, and coriander. Sauté over medium-high heat for 5 minutes, stirring frequently, then reduce the heat to low. Cook, stirring occasionally, until the onion and fennel soften and begin to brown, 10 to 15 minutes.

Add the squash and cook for another 5 minutes. Then add the coconut milk and broth and stir to incorporate fully, increasing the heat to medium. Put on the lid and cook for another 5 minutes, then scoop 1 cup of the liquid (not the onion and fennel) into a bowl. Whisk in the miso, until most clumps are gone. Return the mixture to the pot, reduce the heat to low, and stir to combine. Replace the lid and cook for another 5 minutes.

Transfer to a blender and blend at medium speed until the soup is mostly pureed, with some texture left. Return the soup to the pot and cover.

MAKE THE TOASTED SEEDS

Place the coconut oil in a small frying pan and melt over medium heat. Swirl to coat the pan. Add the sesame and fennel seeds and a sprinkle of salt. Use a spatula to coat the seeds with the oil and let them toast for 2 to 3 minutes, until fragrant. If they start to brown too quickly, remove from the heat. Transfer to a small bowl.

SERVE THE SOUP

Top the soup with a drizzle of coconut milk, the minced fennel fronds, a sprinkle of toasted sesame seeds, and cayenne and salt to taste.

Rhubarb Fennel Ice Cream

I grew up jumping into rivers and pools, scouting waterfalls to jump from, and tiptoeing barefoot down muddy pathways lined with musky white ginger. The verdant scent of jungle breathed life into my lungs, tended to human uncertainties, asserted an animal sense of being. In California, fennel grows wild near highways and rivers and canyons the way white ginger does in Hawaii. Fennel, though, proffers a sweetness that sets it apart from white ginger, a wildness that can be eaten whole.

This sultry blend of jammy red wine, rhubarb, fennel, and cream came to me in the wake of a visit to the Russian River in Sonoma County. We spent days lazing on flat stones, bound to the river by the hum and dip of dragonflies, the rush of reeds in water, and the scent of fennel pollen baking in the summer sun. The river current ran chills through us whenever we got too hot, and we'd return to the table ready for wine and sweetness. Rhubarb's tart, floral brightness is the perfect match for fennel's soft sugar, and wine unites the two. Blended into ice cream, it's a dip into a sweet and tart river of its own kind.

I recommend making a sundae out of it, topped with crushed gingersnaps.

makes about 1 quart
preparation time: overnight ice cream maker
freeze + 40 to 50 minutes + 6 to 7 hours chill time

RHUBARB FENNEL COMPOTE

½ cup jammy red wine (like Shiraz)

⅓ cup honey

½ cup shaved fennel bulb

2 cups chopped rhubarb stalks (leaves discarded)

1 teaspoon lemon zest, plus more for garnish

Pinch of sea salt

ICE CREAM BASE

2½ cups heavy cream

1½ cups whole milk

½ cup honey

½ teaspoon vanilla seeds scraped from the pod, or 1 teaspoon pure vanilla extract

¼ teaspoon sea salt

2 egg yolks

1 cup rhubarb fennel compote

Crushed gingersnaps, for garnish

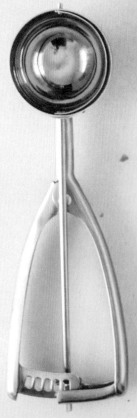

PREPARE YOUR ICE CREAM MAKER

The night before you plan to make the ice cream, freeze the bowl of your ice cream maker.

MAKE THE COMPOTE

In a medium nonreactive saucepan over low heat, stir the wine and honey until fully combined. Add the fennel and rhubarb, and increase the heat until the mixture comes to a boil. Reduce the heat to low and let simmer, uncovered, until the fennel and rhubarb are completely tender, and the compote has thickened, 20 to 25 minutes. Stir in the lemon zest and a pinch of sea salt, and remove from the heat. Let cool completely. Extra compote can be kept in an airtight container in the fridge for up to 1 month.

MAKE THE ICE CREAM

In a large saucepan, whisk the heavy cream, milk, honey, vanilla, salt, and egg yolks. Turn the heat to low and cook, stirring continuously, until the custard reaches 170°F, 20 to 25 minutes—or until it thickens slightly and coats the back of a spoon.

Transfer to a heatproof bowl and cool completely in the fridge, then stir in 1 cup of the cooled rhubarb fennel compote. Freeze in an ice cream maker, according to the manufacturer's instructions, until the consistency is smooth and thick, then transfer to an airtight container. Swirl a few spoonfuls of compote over the top, and freeze for at least 6 hours before eating.

Serve with gingersnaps.

No ice cream maker? The results won't be as refined, but follow the process on page 38.

Fennel Apple Limeade (Vegan)

"And a veggie juice!" one parent would always call to the other, leaning out the open window toward the health food store as I sat fidgeting in the backseat, likely hoping for a frozen malted almond or carob mint soy milk. I learned early on that I did not like my parents' ubiquitous "veggie juice"—a dark and murky blend of carrots, beets, and celery. Little did I know, however, that I would come to love, nay, to crave the once abhorred beverage.

I just needed a few greens and a little citrus in my cup.

When I discovered green juice—I believe it was a blend of greens, apple, celery, lemon, and ginger—I felt like I was drinking milk. My favorite medicinal foods maven, Amanda Chantal Bacon, concurs, calling green juice the *mother's milk of the universe*. This limeade is a fun and fanciful way to get in your greens with no trace of bitterness.

Here, fennel and apple sing together, and lime teases out their sweetness. Celery mellows, and an extra drop or three of stevia (or sweetener of your choice) makes this a juice to blend up at any hour of the day.

serves 1 to 2

preparation time: 7 minutes

1 apple, chilled
⅓ cup sliced fennel bulb
1 (4- to 6-inch) celery stalk, coarsely chopped
2½ tablespoons lime juice

1¾ cups cold water
4 ice cubes
3 drops stevia, or sweetener of choice, as desired

Wash and core the apple, and cut into slices. Place the apple, fennel, celery, lime juice, water, and ice in a blender. Blend on high until fully incorporated. Taste, add the sweetener as desired, then blend again to incorporate. Strain through a fine-mesh strainer, cheesecloth, or nut milk bag.

Pour and drink!

MAKE IT A COCKTAIL!
Gin, vodka, absinthe, St. Germain.

MINT

4

WHEN I WAS EIGHTEEN, a hippie-shaman-man on Maui told me that I needed to spend more time moon-bathing naked under the night sky. I took his advice, for better or worse, and while I can't say it transformed my soul, it did lead to an enduring penchant for being nude outdoors. You can take the girl off the island, but . . .

Mint is an herb that psycho-spiritually urges me to strip off all my clothes and lie naked in beds of its fragrant leaves. Regardless of your nude herbal fantasies (or lack thereof), mint is a kitchen staple as flexible as it is potent. It heightens the tone and expands the depth of any dish graced with its bright, open notes, and it plays exceedingly well with other fresh herbs (think cilantro, basil, and parsley).

Experimenting with mint over the years, I've discovered that it has an expansive quality similar to salt: It enhances other flavors without dominating. In the same way, this little leaf is an excellent friend for healing purposes: It tames nausea, encourages healthy digestion, and will revitalize even the dullest of minds.

Give yourself freedom to get freaky with mint. Try new things. Toss it into dishes you'd never have imagined. You may just find yourself getting naked with it.

Discover more of mint's properties on page 20.

Greek Chopped Salad with Cumin-Fried Chickpeas & Tahini Mint Dressing

My romantic history up to this point may prove that I am better at identifying a perfect salad than I am at finding a perfect partner. Case in point: I first made this salad on a night when I was trying to impress a boy, and while I think it worked, I found myself far more excited about the perfection I'd discovered in my salad bowl than I was about him. Such is the life of a single plant-eater. As enthralled as we both were with my crispy chickpeas, here was another man who was just not quite right.

But the salad—the salad was very, very right. It is, quite simply, my favorite. It's my favorite because it's bold in flavor, it's missing nothing, and it's dense with ingredients yet perfectly sexy in its lightness.

It has wild amounts of mint in it, both in leaf and dressing form, and equally wild amounts of tahini. It has crispy cumin chickpeas that explode with flavor as you nestle into their chewy insides. It has mellow cucumber and sweet tomato and sharp feta. And then there's the grilled pita. And the fact that you can make one perfect bite of every single damn thing.

It's also possible that my love for this salad runs so deep because it's an entire meal in a bowl. It's hot and it's cool and it's salty and it's perfect. Welcome to my dream salad. If you see a man in the shape of this salad, please send him my way.

serves 4

preparation time: 20 minutes

CUMIN-FRIED CHICKPEAS

3 tablespoons olive oil

2 garlic cloves, minced

1 teaspoon ground cumin

1 (15-ounce) can chickpeas, drained

¼ teaspoon sea salt

GREEK CHOPPED SALAD

4½ cups chopped romaine lettuce, stems
    included

1 cup chopped cucumber

1 medium tomato, sliced, seeded, and chopped

½ cup pitted Kalamata olives, quartered

1 cup loosely packed fresh mint leaves, chopped

1 cup chopped or crumbled feta cheese

2 pita rounds (4 to 6 inches)

Olive oil, for toasting pita

TAHINI MINT DRESSING

¼ cup tahini

½ cup water

2 tablespoons olive oil

½ garlic clove

1½ tablespoons lemon juice

¼ teaspoon sea salt

1 to 2 tablespoons fresh mint leaves

MAKE THE CHICKPEAS

In a frying pan, heat the oil over medium
heat. Add the garlic and cumin and stir until
fragrant. Add the chickpeas and salt. Swirl
in the pan and stir to coat the chickpeas
with the oil and spices. Let the chickpeas
cook in an even layer, shaking the pan occasionally, for 5 to 7 minutes, until the skins
are browning and beginning to crisp. When
you start to hear the chickpeas pop, remove
the pan from the heat. Set the chickpeas
aside in a bowl and reserve the seasoned pan
to toast the pita.

MAKE THE SALAD

Place the romaine, cucumber, tomato, olives,
mint, and feta in a large salad bowl.

Drizzle each side of the pitas with
the oil and toast in the seasoned pan over
medium heat for a few minutes on each side,

until the pita begins to crisp. Remove from
the heat and cut the pitas into small trian-
gles to add to the salad. Let cool while you
make the dressing.

MAKE THE DRESSING

Place the tahini, water, oil, garlic, lemon
juice, and salt into a small food processor or
blender and blend until completely smooth.
Add the mint leaves and pulse or blend on
low until they're processed to small flecks.
Alternatively, mince the mint and garlic
and blend all the ingredients by hand with
a whisk.

ASSEMBLE THE SALAD

Add the pita and chickpeas to the salad
bowl, and toss the salad with dressing to
taste. Serve immediately.

Kabocha Coconut Fritters with Pomegranate Mint Raita

Whether I'm in the kitchen or hunched over a notebook, poetry is always at the core of my work. The idea for a dish often arises from a sensory impression—a kind of synesthesia of flavor and feeling that bothers me until I must do something about it. So it was with these fritters. When I was on the phone with a friend who'd recently returned home to India, we began speaking of flavor, of the foods she could find easily nearby. Suddenly, I wanted kabocha coconut fritters, packed with two kinds of coconut and stuffed with feta and mint. Topped with a pomegranate and mint-flecked raita. I was so excited by the idea of the recipe I could hardly wait to try it.

When I actually got into the kitchen to work the recipe through, it was far easier than I had expected. With a good, seasoned cast-iron skillet or frying pan you only need a bit of oil to get truly crisp results.

For the raita, I used a method of heating spices in oil called *tadka*, which was taught to me by my childhood best friend's mother, a beautiful woman from Kerala who made us exquisitely scented curries and breads every weekend. Tempering fenugreek and cumin in hot oil expresses their taste and scent, releases their medicinal properties, and infuses the oil. Swirled into the raita, where it's met by fresh pomegranate, mint, and cool yogurt, it's a dream.

If you can't find kabocha, feel free to use any winter squash of your choosing.

serves 4 to 6

preparation time: about 45 minutes

POMEGRANATE MINT RAITA

1 tablespoon olive oil

¼ teaspoon fenugreek seeds

¼ teaspoon ground cumin

1 cup plain yogurt

1½ teaspoons lime juice

½ teaspoon sea salt

⅓ cup pomegranate arils, plus more for garnish

2 tablespoons chopped fresh mint

KABOCHA COCONUT FRITTERS

1 medium kabocha squash (about 4 cups grated)

¼ cup thinly sliced shallot

3 tablespoons plus 1 teaspoon coconut flour

¾ teaspoon sea salt

1 teaspoon ground cumin

1 teaspoon ground coriander

½ cup chopped fresh mint, plus more for garnish

2 large eggs

½ cup crumbled feta cheese

½ cup unsweetened coconut flakes, plus a few handfuls to toast for garnish

2 tablespoons raw virgin coconut oil

MAKE THE RAITA

Heat the olive oil in a small frying pan over medium heat. Add the fenugreek seeds and cumin and swirl to incorporate. Let the seeds toast for 1 to 2 minutes, until the fenugreek begins to turn golden brown. Remove from the heat.

Combine the yogurt, lime juice, and salt in a bowl. Add most of the pomegranate arils and mint, reserving some to garnish the top. Pour in the olive oil with the toasted spices and swirl all the ingredients together. Top with the remaining pomegranate and mint.

MAKE THE FRITTERS

Cut the squash in half and scoop out the seeds (discard, or wash and toast to snack on). Trim off the stem and base, and use a vegetable peeler to remove the skin. Grate the squash and remove excess moisture by wrapping the squash in a clean kitchen towel and squeezing gently.

In a large bowl, combine the squash, shallot, coconut flour, salt, cumin, coriander, and mint. Whisk the eggs in a separate bowl, and pour into the squash mixture. Stir to incorporate. Fold in the feta and coconut flakes, crumbling some of the coconut flakes if the pieces seem too big.

Line one baking sheet with paper towels, and place another on the middle rack of the oven. Preheat the oven to its lowest setting.

Scoop out ⅓-cup patties of the mixture and flatten to about ¾ inch thick. Let rest on the paper towels while you prepare the pan for frying.

Place the coconut oil in a large frying pan over medium heat. Swirl the pan to evenly distribute the melting oil. After a minute or so, once the oil shimmers, test the oil with a droplet of water. If it sizzles, it's ready. Use a spatula to transfer the fritters to the pan, leaving 1 to 2 inches between patties. Cook for 4 to 5 minutes, then flip and cook for 3 to 4 minutes on the other side. When the outside bits are crisp and the fritters are starting to brown, remove from the pan and place on the baking sheet in the oven. Continue until finished, adding more coconut oil if necessary. Once finished, toast a few handfuls of coconut flakes in the pan, over low heat, until just golden (they toast quickly!).

Serve the fritters topped with raita, more fresh mint, pomegranate arils, and the toasted coconut flakes.

Burrata Artichoke Tartines with Roasted Lemon Mint Pesto

These adorable little toasts are a paean to my arrival in Los Angeles, and the first meal I ever had at Gjelina. I was still discovering the thrum of LA, navigating my love-hate relationship with it, the way its concrete vibrates with creativity, the way the heat crawls along the asphalt, the way everyone constantly strives to be better, thinner, prettier, cooler, brighter, smarter, sexier, truthier. I tumbled through the rough and chic beach streets of Venice to meet a friend as instructed, at a place that was then simply another restaurant with two consecutive consonants in its name.

But then Gjelina opened its doors to me, swallowed me up in its cool metal and glass and midnight-blue tones and fed me the best food I'd ever tasted. There was a complexity to its vegetables that summoned me to show up for plant life in a way I never had before. And yes, I'll admit: There was a lot of burrata—that creamier, fairer, far richer cousin to mozzarella.

These toasts are an ode to that afternoon, the magic of finding beauty within heat and dust and asphalt and dreams. Roasting lemon simultaneously strengthens its citrus flavor and mellows its acid; when paired with mint and hazelnuts, this pesto is the perfect vehicle for the mild salt of burrata and artichoke.

serves 4
preparation time: 35 minutes

ROASTED LEMON MINT PESTO

½ medium lemon, washed, thinly sliced, and
    seeded

¼ cup plus 3 tablespoons olive oil

1 cup fresh mint leaves

¼ cup toasted hazelnuts or almonds

2 garlic cloves

¼ teaspoon sea salt

BURRATA ARTICHOKE TARTINES

½ baguette or loaf bread of choice, thickly sliced

Olive oil, for drizzling

8 ounces burrata cheese

½ cup artichoke hearts in oil

Small fresh mint leaves, for garnish

Crushed red pepper flakes, to taste

MAKE THE PESTO

Preheat the oven to 450°F. Line a small
baking sheet with parchment paper and
lay the lemon slices in a single layer on the
sheet. Drizzle with 1 tablespoon of the oil.
Roast for 15 to 17 minutes, until the juices
are tacky and the lemons are beginning to
caramelize. Let cool for 10 minutes, then
transfer to a small food processor, add the
remaining ¼ cup plus 2 tablespoons oil, the
mint, hazelnuts, garlic, and salt and blend
until you have a very lightly chunky pesto.

MAKE THE TARTINES

Gently toast the sliced baguette or bread to
the desired crispness. Drizzle with oil, dollop
with burrata, add an artichoke heart or two,
top with pesto, and finish with a couple of
fresh mint leaves and red pepper flakes.

Fresh Mint & Olive Oil Ice Cream with Apricots

Perhaps the sweetest discovery of my life in the kitchen is the power of the perfect singular ingredient. If the apricot is in fine form, it needs little else to express itself in astonishingly poetic ways. This simple approach to flavor—placing ingredients first—was bestowed upon us by culinary giant Alice Waters, whose earth-connected brilliance inspired me more than ever as I returned to California, the state we both call home.

To this day, there is one unique flavor symphony that always takes my breath away: fruit + mint + honey + olive oil + sea salt.

Perhaps it's that it hits a home run of tastes, uniting sweet, salty, acidic, fatty, and bitter in one fell swoop. Or perhaps it's that it tastes like a humid summer night with fireflies teasing at your breath and thunderstorms threatening to burst overhead. Or perhaps it's just a communion of flavor that humans were meant to discover all along because it is perfect. Whatever it may be, I had to make an ice cream sundae out of it.

Welcome to fresh mint and olive oil ice cream with apricots and sea salt: This is about as backyard wild as dessert gets.

makes 1 quart
preparation time: overnight ice cream maker
freeze + 40 minutes + 7 to 8 hours chill time

FRESH MINT AND OLIVE OIL ICE CREAM

2½ cups heavy cream

1½ cups whole milk

½ cup honey

½ teaspoon vanilla seeds scraped from the pod, or 1 teaspoon pure vanilla extract

2 pinches sea salt

4 cups fresh mint leaves, washed and dried

2 tablespoons olive oil

2 egg yolks

ICE CREAM TOPPINGS

Sliced fresh apricots or other stone fruit

Olive oil, for drizzling

2 tablespoons fresh mint leaves, chiffonaded or finely chopped

Flaky sea salt, to taste

PREPARE YOUR ICE CREAM MAKER

The night before you plan to make the ice cream, freeze the bowl of your ice cream maker.

MAKE THE ICE CREAM

Heat the heavy cream, milk, honey, vanilla, and salt in a large saucepan over medium heat, whisking until steam rises. Slightly crush the mint leaves and immerse them in the liquid to allow them to release their oils. Cover the saucepan, remove from the heat, and let steep for 20 to 30 minutes, then strain out the mint and transfer the mixture to an airtight container and let cool completely in the fridge.

When you're ready to make the ice cream, whisk the oil and egg yolks into the cooled, strained ice cream base. Return to the stove, and cook in a large saucepan over low heat, stirring continuously, until the custard reaches 170°F, 20 to 25 minutes—or until it thickens slightly and coats the back of a spoon.

Transfer to a heatproof bowl, cover, and cool completely in the fridge. Freeze in the ice cream maker, according to the manufacturer's instructions, until the consistency is smooth and thick, then transfer to an airtight container and freeze for at least 6 hours before eating.

No ice cream maker? The results won't be as refined, but follow the process on page 38.

Serve the ice cream with apricots, a drizzle of oil, mint, and a sprinkle of flaky sea salt.

Cantaloupe Mint Smoothie (Vegan)

I grew up in a culture obsessed with health and cleansing long before it had reached mainstream America. My parents did seasonal cleanses, spiked their water with spirulina, and meditated. There was nary a sugary cereal in our cabinets, and I wasn't allowed to eat chocolate until I was six. Though I'm infinitely grateful for my early immersion in real food, it also meant that I harbored a good deal of fear about eating foods I considered unhealthy. I saw my perennially rail-thin mother as the epitome of all things healthful, her rigid diet the gold standard to which I assumed I should aspire.

When she got sick, though, something in me was freed to do things differently. To know that imperfection was inevitable, that control and fear were never the answer. That food should be about joy more than anything else. And so I started to eat intuitively, in ways that honored both my whims and my needs for basic, vital nourishment.

Now, when I feel the need for a reset, I simplify my diet and spend more time with delicious whole foods, like this smoothie. It tastes as indulgent as a shake, but it will set your cells to celebrating rather than combusting in a sugar crash. The lime removes any cloying sweetness from the cantaloupe, and the ginger amplifies the fruit's complexity. Mint comes around to elevate the entire flavor profile.

This is the perfect drink to make as a hot afternoon snack or a quick morning pick-me-up. Melons contain hefty amounts of vitamins A and C and are full of lycopene, all of which help eliminate free radicals and regenerate the body's tissues. Ginger serves as an anti-inflammatory, and mint will freshen your perspective and soothe a finicky belly.

serves 1 to 2

preparation time: 5 minutes

½ large chilled cantaloupe, seeds and flesh scooped out, or 2 cups frozen

½ lime, peeled and seeded

1 tablespoon finely grated ginger, or to taste

4 ice cubes, cracked

15 fresh mint leaves

Place the cantaloupe in a blender. Add the lime, ginger, and ice cubes to the blender and blend until smooth. Add the mint and blend or pulse on low until the leaves are broken down into small flecks.

Pour and drink!

MAKE IT A COCKTAIL!
Rum, vodka.

Mint Awakening Spritz

Let's talk hydrosols. A hydrosol is a water distillation of a plant, such that the water is imbued with the essence of the plant, its fragrance and its healing properties. In the years I lived on Maui after college, I discovered the power of hydrosols in tandem with essential oils. One of the world's foremost essential oil and hydrosol distillation teams had moved to Maui, and I reaped the benefits of getting to know their products. I became the glad recipient of fresh batches of jojoba-macerated white ginger lily, Himalayan lavender, and Kashmir rose.

And then there were the hydrosols: Waters of cedar and spruce and cypress provided strength, mandarin and vanilla sweetened, rose gave me ease. I used these as body and atmospheric sprays as often as I added them directly to water and juices to drink. There was a potent intimacy to bringing the plant distillations directly into my body.

While I don't know (slash am too impatient for) the art of distillation, this spritz is an easy way to mimic the effects of a hydrosol. Mint soothes digestion and awakens even the sleepiest of minds and bodies. This spritz can be used on face and body, or as a room spray to freshen any environment.

makes 8 ounces
preparation time: 5 minutes

8 ounces water

2 drops culinary-grade peppermint essential oil, or 1 cup gently crushed fresh mint leaves

Combine the water and essential oil in a clean, sanitized spray bottle. If using fresh mint leaves, let sit for at least an hour, refrigerated, before use. Shake vigorously before each use. Store refrigerated for up to 3 days if using fresh mint, and 6 months if using essential oil.

Coconut Mint Salt Scrub

On weekends, when we weren't in dance rehearsal or reading Woolf or hanging out at the beach, my childhood BFF Tara and I would regularly slather ourselves with homemade DIYs. The event always began with a good forage, and then we'd sort out whatever banana, papaya, and hibiscus we'd found and determine the course of our spa day. One of our most epic concoctions was a pure banana mash, which we relished joyfully until we discovered it was as much a skin emollient as an insect aphrodisiac. We washed it off quickly and crushed conditioning hibiscus leaves into our hair with newly softened palms instead.

These mornings formed the blueprint of my approach to body care, and this coconut mint scrub is a direct, albeit more refined, descendant.

Where some people advise to put the lime in the coconut, I say put the mint in the coconut and add some salt and coconut oil and shake it all up. And then scrub it all over your body.

This scrub evokes a more recent summer spent with friends and their kids on Lake Tahoe, where we scrubbed ourselves clean at the lakefront and then sunned our quenched skin in the bright, clear light of the Sierras. Grinding the coconut makes it a finer match for the salt's exfoliation, and coconut oil is a beautiful emollient for skin that's sloughed off. Fresh mint leaves release their oils as they're crushed, producing cooling menthol to tone skin and clear a cloudy mind.

Skin is left glowing with rejuvenation and moisture.

makes about 1 cup
preparation time: 5 minutes

⅓ cup finely shredded unsweetened dried
    coconut

⅓ cup sea salt

2 tablespoons raw virgin coconut oil, melted
    and cooled

⅔ cup fresh mint leaves, minced

Divide the shredded coconut in half, and process half of it in a small food processor, herb mill, or (clean) coffee grinder until the coconut pieces are about half the size, and some of the coconut is powdery, 15 to 30 seconds depending on the strength of your grinder.

In a small bowl, combine the two types of shredded coconut with the salt and oil. Gently toss in the mint, massaging to release the scent.

The scrub keeps for a day or two in the fridge, until the mint loses its freshness. Do not use on the face or on previously irritated skin. Bring to room temperature before using, to soften the coconut oil.

Use in the shower, with a drain catch that will filter out the bits of mint and coconut. You can also put a paper towel or washcloth over the drain to catch these bits and make cleanup easier.

5

OREGANO

THE WORD *oregano* comes from the Latin *oros*—mountain—and *ganos*—joy. Mountain joy is the perfect way to describe my earliest memories of the herb that, for me, most fully embodied the concept of edible landscaping. My parents spent years as landscape architects of the beautiful property we called home, and my mother embedded as much of it as she could with edible plants. So when we needed oregano to make a pasta or a dip, she'd send me down the front porch to the yard, where birds of paradise and orchids cozied up to sprawling stands of rosemary and a hardy ground cover of oregano.

In subsequent years, I got to know oregano in entirely new ways. I discovered Mexican oregano, delicious with beans and cumin, and giant, furry-leaved Caribbean oregano. And then I discovered oregano's power as medicine.

I spent most of my life quite healthy—I had taken antibiotics only once until the age of twenty-four—but in the weeks before my mother died, and in the years after, my body rebelled in shock and grief. Eight days before she died, I woke feeling like someone had shoved a dagger into the farthest recesses of my throat. Our family doctor prescribed antibiotics, and I made it through to the other side of the strep throat or whatever psychosomatic trauma had lodged itself in my shocked and tenderized body.

I would get sick again and again after my mom died, my lungs growing brutally congested. During that plague of grief I discovered a new side to oregano: its medicinal properties concentrated in oregano oil.

Though you would need to consume tremendous amounts of oregano for medicinal use, the herb contains potent antiviral properties and rosmarinic acid, a compound that acts as a powerful antioxidant agent. On the skin, oregano tones and tightens, soothing irritation, infection, and inflammation.

Discover more of oregano's properties on page 21.

White Bean Yogurt Dip with Warm Citrus Olives & Herby Flatbread

We do not always make friends at the high points in our lives. So it was that, though I'd known Suryamayi for years, our friendship solidified at a moment of tremendous flux for us both. We found ourselves together in a new city, willing ourselves to move forward with the studious self-consciousness of two young people who'd spent excessive amounts of time on meditation retreats. Like me, Suri had grown up with western yogi parents. Luckily, we knew how to laugh at each other (and ourselves) in our seriousness as much as we sought out ways to support each other in healing.

This recipe was one that morphed out of our time together, one late summer evening in San Francisco. I might have asked for a hummus of some sort, and Suri's intuitive kitchen moves led her to whip up a glorious, garlicky white bean dip made with a generous hand of tangy yogurt. I was smitten.

This version adds oregano to the mix to counter the sharpness of garlic and yogurt, and provide aromatic depth. Warm citrus olives are incredibly easy, yet feel like a true luxury. Heating citrus peel releases its fragrance and its oils, touching the salty olives with a perfect floral tang. Herby flatbread, ideal for scooping and sandwiching, rounds out this trio. Serve this as an appetizer for a crowd or whip up a batch to give you lunch for a week.

Let it give you strength to change, and to laugh in the process.

serves 4
preparation time: 20 to 25 minutes

WHITE BEAN YOGURT DIP

2 tablespoons olive oil

2 garlic cloves, quartered

2 (15-ounce) cans cannellini beans, rinsed and drained (about 3½ cups)

¼ cup plus 2 tablespoons plain yogurt

2 teaspoons lemon juice

1 teaspoon sea salt

Freshly cracked black pepper, to taste

Fresh oregano leaves, for garnish

WARM CITRUS OLIVES

2 tablespoons olive oil

2 tablespoons thinly sliced lemon peel

1 teaspoon fresh oregano leaves

½ cup olives of choice (such as Castelvetrano, Kalamata, or Greek), drained

HERBY FLATBREAD

3 tablespoons olive oil

1 garlic clove, crushed

1 teaspoon lemon zest

1 teaspoon fresh oregano leaves

Flaky sea salt, to taste

Crushed red pepper flakes, to taste

Bread of choice (such as pita, naan, loaf bread, or homemade from pizza dough recipe on page 119)

MAKE THE DIP

Warm the oil in a small saucepan over medium heat. Add the garlic and sauté until fragrant, gently shaking the pan to prevent sticking. Remove from the heat when the garlic is beginning to turn golden at the edges.

Place the beans, yogurt, lemon juice, salt, and a few dashes of pepper in a food processor or blender. Pour in the oil and garlic. Blend until completely smooth, then adjust the salt as desired and transfer to a serving dish. Garnish with fresh oregano leaves.

MAKE THE OLIVES

Heat the oil in a small saucepan over low heat. Add the lemon peel and oregano and let the oil infuse for 1 to 2 minutes, occasionally shaking the pan. Add the olives and warm gently, shaking the pan or stirring, another 1 to 2 minutes. Remove from the heat and let sit in the pan to keep warm until ready to serve. When ready to serve, pour the contents of the pan into a small serving bowl.

MAKE THE FLATBREAD

Mix the oil, garlic, lemon zest, oregano, salt, and red pepper flakes in a small bowl. Slice the bread and brush the oil mixture onto the bread with a pastry brush or drizzle with a spoon.

Grill the bread in an oiled 12-inch frying pan or cast-iron skillet over medium heat, giving each side 1 to 2 minutes, until it begins to crisp and brown.

Remove from the heat and serve immediately, with bowls of white bean yogurt dip and warm citrus olives.

Balsamic Lentils with Roasted Eggplant, Tomatoes & Oregano Cream (Vegan)

When I lived in Avignon, France, for a summer, I landed in the home of a French Moroccan woman named Nadja, who possessed a kind of irrepressible sexiness born of the right habits, done in the right light, solidified into amber beauty over many years. With her I had my first *yaourt de soja* (soy yogurt), with her I discovered that the only way to learn another language was to completely and utterly immerse myself in it. Somehow, through the lens of her life in that golden city of heat and smoke, Nadja made me feel it was okay to be myself. Pre-Beyoncé, Nadja was my original icon of single-lady power.

This time also affirmed my fixation with the nightshades: Eggplants and tomatoes became layered ratatouilles, tender with salt and oil and herbs. We ate them with cheeses and breads. We did not hesitate to drench them in butter. We did not hesitate to pair them with wine. And my goodness, we certainly did not shy away from eating these nightshades, as is now the trend in some diets. The French approach taught me a voraciousness of appetite previously unknown to my restraint-oriented New Age palate. And showed me that evenings of indulgence can be followed by mornings of soy yogurt.

This dish is a simple ode to my time in France, to easy indulgence. To just being me. Paired with balsamic lentils, it's my favorite kind of meal. And as a creamy vegan hat tip to Nadja, I've used my friend Sherrie's vegan hemp and cashew base to make an oregano cream to top it all off.

serves 2 to 4

preparation time: about 55 minutes

OREGANO CREAM

⅓ cup water

½ teaspoon red wine vinegar

1 tablespoon hemp seeds

¼ cup raw cashews

¼ teaspoon sea salt, plus more to taste

¼ teaspoon granulated onion

¼ teaspoon ground black pepper

1 teaspoon fresh oregano leaves

BALSAMIC LENTILS

1½ cups dry French green (Le Puy) lentils, rinsed

5 cups water or vegetable broth, for cooking the lentils

2 large garlic cloves, scored

1 onion, halved and thinly sliced

3 tablespoons olive oil

3 tablespoons balsamic vinegar

1 teaspoon salt, plus a few pinches

ROASTED EGGPLANT AND TOMATOES

¾ pound eggplant, washed, trimmed, and cut into ½-inch slices

Sea salt

5 medium tomatoes, washed and trimmed

3 garlic cloves, coarsely chopped

1 tablespoon minced shallot

1 tablespoon fresh oregano leaves, coarsely chopped, plus more for garnish

¼ cup plus 1 tablespoon olive oil

½ teaspoon salt

½ teaspoon red wine vinegar

¼ teaspoon freshly cracked black pepper, plus more for garnish

¼ cup raw pine nuts, toasted in a dry skillet until golden brown

MAKE THE CREAM

Place the water, red wine vinegar, hemp seeds, cashews, salt, onion, and pepper in a small food processor or blender and blend until completely smooth. Add the oregano leaves and pulse until they're small flecks. Pour into an airtight container, cover, and place in the fridge while you make the rest of the dish.

MAKE THE LENTILS

Place the rinsed lentils, the water, and the garlic in a medium pot. Cover with a lid, bring to a boil, and then reduce the heat to low. Simmer until the lentils are completely soft, yet still holding their shape, an additional 20 to 25 minutes. When done, drain the lentils and discard the garlic.

While the lentils are cooking, place the onion, 2 tablespoons of the oil, and 2 tablespoons of the balsamic vinegar in a large frying pan. Add a few pinches of salt. Sauté on medium heat, stirring occasionally, until the onion is deep brown and has reduced significantly, 20 to 25 minutes depending on the heat. Some of the onion may even become crisp and caramelized. Remove from the heat.

Empty the drained lentils into the frying pan with the onion and mix, adding the remaining 1 tablespoon each oil and balsamic vinegar, and the 1 teaspoon salt. Incorporate and check for taste. Adjust the salt, oil, and balsamic vinegar until the salt, acid, sweet, and fat flavors are well balanced for your palate.

MAKE THE EGGPLANT AND TOMATO

Preheat the oven to 450°F. Line a large rimmed baking sheet with paper towels. Spread the eggplant slices in a single layer on the baking sheet. Sprinkle with the sea salt, gently massaging the salt into all areas of the eggplant. (Salting the eggplant draws out excess water, resulting in a creamier texture once cooked.) Let sit for 10 to 15 minutes, then squeeze out the excess water into paper towels. Line the baking sheet with parchment paper, and return the eggplant slices to the sheet, laying them in a single layer with a bit of space between each.

Trim the tomatoes and slice in half, removing the seeds with your fingers. Slice the tomatoes into wedges and lay them on the baking sheet between the eggplant slices. Sprinkle the eggplant and tomatoes with the garlic, shallot, and oregano. Drizzle with the oil and sprinkle with ½ teaspoon salt.

Roast for 20 to 25 minutes, until the tomatoes are bubbling and the veggies are browning at the edges.

Remove from the oven and transfer to a serving dish. Toss with the red wine vinegar, pepper, and pine nuts.

Serve the lentils topped with the roasted eggplant, tomatoes, and pine nuts, drizzled with the oregano cream. Garnish with fresh oregano and freshly cracked black pepper to taste.

Capellini Pomodoro with Homemade Ricotta

There are a few dishes in these pages that are straight-up, absolute comfort foods. This is one of them. I've always loved capellini—angel hair pasta—its tenderness, its ability to soak up oil and garlic, the way it twirls so easily around a fork. Paired with a fast, fresh marinara and homemade ricotta, this is the sweetest, simplest, classiest way to dress up pasta. It screams sexy night in—I mean, hellur, you just made ricotta *from scratch*. How hot is that? (And yes, you can have sexy nights in with yourself. I call them Every Day of My Life.)

It's almost laughable how easy it is to make the marinara and the ricotta, neither of which you'd typically think to whip up at home. I promise you, though, you'll only do just that from this point forward. Fresh marinara, anchored by sweet marjoram (a cousin to oregano), garlic, and, yes, oregano, will make your knees weak. No fancy culinary technique required.

And to make ricotta you need only be skilled enough to stir lemon juice into heated milk and cream. Game? I thought so. Welcome to the homemade comfort food club.

nota bene: Because this is a simple dish, select the best tomatoes and pasta you can find so that their flavors truly shine. You can use leftover marinara and ricotta on pizza—you'll be happy you did.

serves 4 to 6
preparation time: about 1 hour

MARINARA

¼ cup olive oil

3 garlic cloves, crushed or minced

2 tablespoons fresh oregano leaves, plus more
for garnish

1 tablespoon fresh marjoram (or additional
oregano) leaves, plus more for garnish

3 pounds tomatoes, washed, trimmed, cored,
lightly seeded, and coarsely chopped

1 teaspoon sea salt

1½ teaspoons balsamic vinegar

¼ teaspoon crushed red pepper flakes, plus more
for garnish

HOMEMADE RICOTTA

4 cups whole milk

2 cups heavy cream

1 teaspoon sea salt

⅓ cup lemon juice

1 small garlic clove, minced

8 ounces dried capellini pasta

MAKE THE MARINARA

In a large stockpot, heat the oil over
medium heat. Stir in the garlic, oregano,
and marjoram and continue stirring until
fragrant. Add the tomatoes and stir to
incorporate. As the tomatoes begin to
break down, stir in the salt. Bring to a boil.
Reduce the heat to low and add the vinegar
and red pepper flakes. Let simmer for 20
to 30 minutes with a lid partially covering
the pot to allow steam to escape, stirring
occasionally. Turn off the heat when the
sauce has reduced by about half and the oil
shimmers orange on the surface.

MAKE THE RICOTTA

Set a large mesh sieve inside a large heatproof glass bowl. Line the sieve with 2 layers
of cheesecloth and set in the sink.

Bring the milk, heavy cream, and sea
salt to a boil in a large nonreactive (stainless
steel or enamel) stockpot. As soon as it
boils, remove from the heat and stir in the
lemon juice until just combined. Let sit for
2 minutes, until the curds separate from
the whey. Pour into the lined sieve and let
drain for 15 to 20 minutes, or longer for
a thicker ricotta. When drained to your
liking, transfer the cheese into a small bowl
and stir in the garlic.

When you are ready to serve, cook the pasta
according to the package directions, drain,
and add sauce to your liking. Top with dol-
lops of ricotta and an extra sprinkle of red
pepper flakes and marjoram, if desired.

Oatmeal Oregano Purifying Mask

I grew up thinking I was just like my mother—supremely sensitive to just about everything seen and unseen in the environment surrounding me. I thought, and the world reinforced, that we were twinned in our interior constitutions, our tender ways of being, our delicate feelings, our propensity to turn inward rather than out.

I spent time protecting myself, being overly careful, concerned that if I exposed myself I would be as susceptible to the harshness of the world as she had been. I, like her, spent much of my young life asserting my otherness, seeking refuge in a strong inner life, in Bach flower tinctures and homeopathic remedies and pendulums. It wasn't until she died that I realized I was, in many ways, not at all like her.

I was quiet, yes, but I was also loud and wild and a different kind of sensitive. I wanted to go to Jay Z and Beyoncé concerts and sometimes eat French fries and be younger rather than older. Perhaps, suddenly, I was just myself—in all my quietness and my loudness.

Even still, in the quiet moments, I found that I called upon my mother's wisdom for balance, for guidance back to equilibrium. In the frenzy of too much, when anxiety is high, I turn to plants for reprieve. And, when stress takes its toll on my skin, I turn to oatmeal and oregano, as she taught me.

Oatmeal has tremendous power to ameliorate skin irritation, slough off dead skin, and soften the new skin revealed. The finer you grind your oats, the gentler this mask will be. Sweet almond oil and fresh oregano turn this mask into a bit of a poultice, which can be used to draw out impurities and tame troublesome skin conditions.

nota bene: If you double the recipe, you can use the mixture in the bath, creating an ideal environment for soaking and relief.

makes enough for 3 to 4 uses
preparation time: 5 minutes

½ cup rolled oats
3 tablespoons minced fresh oregano leaves

1 tablespoon sweet almond oil
¼ cup water, plus more as needed

Grind the oats and oregano for about
30 seconds in a (clean) spice or coffee
grinder, until they're floury. Transfer to a
small bowl and mix in the oil. Use as is
for a scrub. For a mask, stir in the water
until the mixture becomes creamy.

As a mask, apply a tablespoonful or
more to the face and let dry, then rinse
off. As a scrub, use in the shower, on
the face and body. If you use in the
bath, the water will turn milky with oat
flour and be perfumed with oregano,
resulting in skin softening, soothing,
and purifying.

ROSEMARY

6

THROUGH BILLOWING LINEN and a mind already slowed by the trade winds, I make out rows and rows of grapes in the vineyard next door, light filtering through towering avocado trees outside, the sweet smell of earth all around me. No cars. No sirens. No people. Just sunlight diffused through rosemary and citrus blossoms.

This is Ulupalakua—"the place where the breadfruit ripens" in Hawaiian— so named for the cowboys who lugged the fruit from Hana, in the east, to this southern outpost on the slopes of Haleakala Crater. By the time they arrived in Ulu, as we call it for short, they could scoop the fibrous flesh out of its bulbous green encasement. Ulupalakua was, and still is, a fertile land.

And I'm finally home. Home for Thanksgiving. Home to be with family. Home to take refuge in the ocean. Home to be grateful for this place that nourishes so deeply. Home to pick lemons and rosemary.

This stimulating herb is revered for its ability to rouse and tone tissue, brain and otherwise, while perfuming the palate with an herbaceous glow. It also holds the sweetness of one of my last memories of my mother: When she could still walk, touching the rosemary in our front yard's garden, her hair glowing amber from the sun setting into the ocean just ahead.

Discover more of rosemary's properties on page 21.

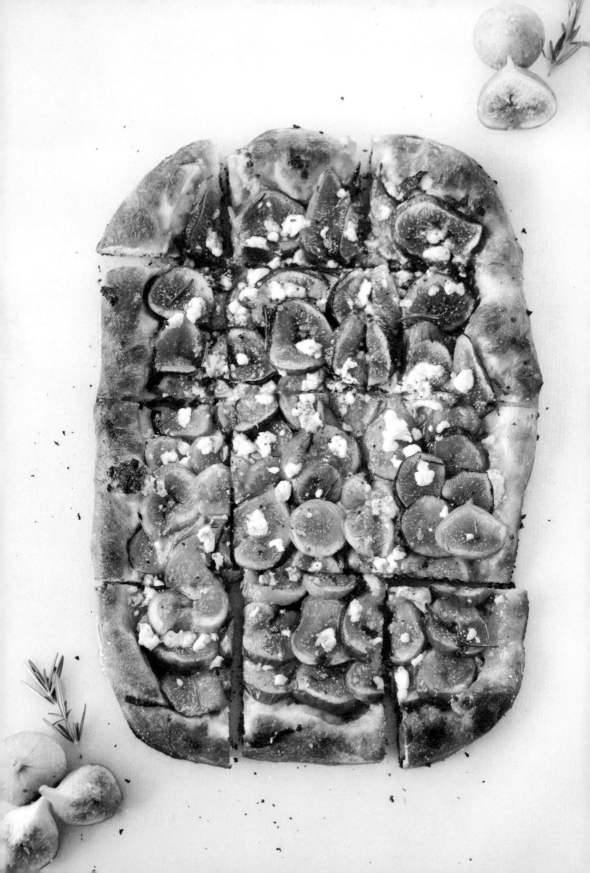

Roasted Fig Pizza with Rosemary Chèvre & Balsamic Caramelized Onion

For two days, I was obsessed with thoughts of this pizza. It came to me in a shamanic reverie (aka, scrolling through my Facebook feed for recipe ideas), and I knew I had to make it. It was so easy, so possible, and would be so delicious. I started frantically texting people: "Do you want to come over and make this roasted fig, chèvre, and caramelized onion pizza?" The answers were inevitably the same: first the expected "LOL," and then, as the obsession began to infiltrate, "YES. WHEN?"

We set a date. I had everything I needed, and would go to my favorite local bakery for pre-made dough. I picked rosemary on my daily stroll around the neighborhood, and made sure said friends were bringing wine and chocolate. Culinary heaven ensued—well, I thought it was culinary heaven until Janson, my partner in kitchen crime, decided to drizzle truffle oil on it. And then, my friends, this pizza officially arrived. We may or may not have eaten the entire thing in one sitting.

The key is in the alchemy of balsamic caramelized onions and oven-roasted figs commingling with rosemary. It's a combination that perfectly bridges sweet and savory, a solvent for life's complexity.

makes 1 large or 2 smaller pizzas
preparation time: about 35 minutes + 3 to 4 hours if making your own pizza dough

PIZZA DOUGH

(or 16 ounces store-bought pizza dough, at room temperature)

1⅓ cups lukewarm water

1½ teaspoons active dry yeast

2 teaspoons extra-virgin olive oil, plus more for the bowl

3 cups plus 1 tablespoon all-purpose flour, plus more as needed

2 teaspoons kosher or sea salt, plus more for sprinkling

PIZZA TOPPINGS

1 large yellow onion, thinly sliced

2 tablespoons olive oil, plus more for drizzling

2 to 3 tablespoons balsamic vinegar, plus more for drizzling

½ teaspoon sea salt, plus more to taste

¼ teaspoon freshly cracked black pepper, plus more to taste

Cornmeal, for the pizza stone or baking sheet

4 to 5 ounces chèvre (goat cheese)

1 tablespoon chopped fresh rosemary leaves

8 to 10 ripe Mission or Turkish figs, sliced ¼ inch thick

Truffle oil, for drizzling (optional)

MAKE THE DOUGH

Start the pizza dough 3 to 4 hours ahead. In a small bowl, combine the water, yeast, and oil. In a large bowl, whisk together the flour and salt. Add the wet ingredients to the dry and knead the dough until the mixture comes together into a ball, smooth but a bit tacky to the touch. Add more flour if the dough is too wet. Transfer the dough to a floured surface and knead for 3 minutes to create a smooth ball. Cover with a dish towel and let the dough rest for 15 minutes, then knead for another 3 minutes.

Transfer the dough to a well-oiled bowl and cover with a damp dish towel. Place in a warm location, or if your kitchen is cold, inside your oven. Let rise for 3 to 4 hours. Once the dough is doubled in size, roll it into a ball. (Cut the dough in half and form into 2 balls if making 2 pizzas.) Will keep in the fridge for 2 weeks, or in the freezer for up to 3 weeks. Bring to room temperature before using.

MAKE THE PIZZA

Preheat the oven to 525°F. In a large frying pan on medium heat, sauté the onion in the olive oil and vinegar, sprinkling with the salt and pepper. Continue stirring until the onion is soft, transparent, and browning, 20 to 25 minutes. Taste and add more salt and vinegar as necessary. The onion should be tangy and umami-filled.

Sprinkle a large pizza stone or baking sheet with cornmeal and stretch 1 large ball or 2 smaller balls of dough by letting them hang from both hands until they reach the desired shape and evenness. The edges can be slightly thicker than the middle, and the whole thing should be quite thin, as it will rise. It's a pretty forgiving piece of dough, so don't worry too much. If making 2 pizzas, divide all the ingredients in half.

Drizzle the dough with a generous hand of olive oil and a sprinkle of salt, then evenly spread out the caramelized onion. Crumble most of the cheese and sprinkle most of the rosemary on top. Arrange the figs in a single layer, top with the rest of the cheese and rosemary, and drizzle vinegar over it all.

Bake for 10 to 15 minutes, checking occasionally. Remove from the oven when the edges are golden brown and crisp to your liking. Transfer to a wooden cutting board, add a drizzle of truffle oil if you choose, and cut for serving.

Rosemary & Sharp Cheddar Corn Bread

Skillet corn breads evoke for me an alternate version of myself that lives on a ranch in Montana and cooks everything over a wood-burning stove with weathered, hand-carved spoons and a perpetually steaming cauldron of herbs bubbling in the background. Truth be told, I've never been to Montana, but the wilds of ranch land around my childhood home boasted many a remote cabin.

We overnighted in them often as middle- and high-schoolers, spending cold mountain evenings under stars that glittered unstoppably. We listened to the cows and felt the bracing evening dew against our skin and warmed ourselves by fires before playing rounds of (very tame) truth or dare. Alas, there were no wood-burning stoves or skillet corn breads in sight, but I emerged from this formative era with half my heart out on the ranch.

To this day, I dream of a future home with land in all directions, and no concrete in sight. And, of course, a steady supply of buttery skillet corn bread.

This uniquely egg-free corn bread is quite light, making use of water and apple cider vinegar in place of heavier buttermilk. Don't worry though, it's loaded with melty cheddar and richly aromatic rosemary.

Serve this with butter and honey, hot from the oven. It's delicious as a savory-sweet breakfast addition, or alongside a savory soup for lunch or dinner.

serves 6 to 8

preparation time: 35 to 40 minutes

1 cup yellow cornmeal

1 cup all-purpose unbleached flour

1½ teaspoons baking powder

¼ teaspoon baking soda

½ teaspoon sea salt

1 tablespoon fresh rosemary leaves

⅓ cup brown sugar, packed

1 cup water

1½ teaspoons apple cider vinegar

¼ cup safflower oil or other vegetable oil

1½ cups grated sharp cheddar cheese

Salted butter, for serving

Honey, for serving

Preheat the oven to 350°F. Oil a 9-inch cast-iron skillet or similarly sized baking pan.

In a large bowl, whisk the cornmeal, flour, baking powder, baking soda, salt, and rosemary.

In a medium bowl, whisk the sugar, water, vinegar, and oil. Add the wet ingredients to the dry and stir with a silicone spatula until just mixed. Fold in ¾ cup of the cheese. Do not overmix. Pour into the skillet and gently smooth the top.

Bake for 20 minutes or until the center is lightly browned and a knife comes out clean. Remove from the oven and turn the broiler on low. Sprinkle the remaining ¾ cup cheese over the top. Place the skillet directly under the broiler for 2 to 4 minutes, until the cheese is bubbly and turning golden. Remove from the broiler and let cool for a few minutes, then serve with butter and honey, as desired. Serve while still hot for optimum flavor.

Sweet Orange & Rosemary Cream Pops with Salty Chocolate Drizzle

Growing up, I spent hours playing in the orchards around our home. Some were ours, some were our neighbors', and I ran freely among all of them; there were no fences to separate one property from the other. Our closest neighbors, Fig and Serena (yes, their actual names), often hosted me for afternoon tea and toast, sending me home with T-shirts full of navel oranges warm from the sun. Their oranges were the best, irrepressibly sweet yet soaring with strong acidity. They remain, to this day, my optimal orange.

Fig and Serena no longer live on that property, but I occasionally sneak an orange or two from those trees. These pops are the salty-sweet-tangy embodiment of those afternoons: the sun, the citrus, the scent of the land, the generosity of friends, the open sky of childhood.

And of course, there's that salty, dark chocolate drizzle: Making it takes just a few moments and requires no special skills whatsoever. It's merely a fast way to slather dark chocolate all over your dessert. Begin here, and let it change your life.

makes 6 pops
preparation time: about 4 hours

ORANGE AND ROSEMARY CREAM POPS

⅓ cup honey

4 sprigs fresh rosemary plus 1½ teaspoons chopped rosemary leaves

1½ cups orange segments, seeds and pith removed

½ cup heavy cream

¼ cup Greek yogurt

SALTY CHOCOLATE DRIZZLE

½ cup bittersweet chocolate, chopped or as chips

1½ teaspoons raw coconut oil

2 pinches sea salt

POP TOPPINGS

Flaky sea salt

Fresh rosemary leaves, finely chopped

Orange zest

MAKE THE POPS

Place the honey in a small saucepan over low heat. Add the sprigs of rosemary and stir as the honey softens. Bring to a simmer, and then remove from the heat. Let sit for at least 30 minutes (and up to 2 hours, for a stronger rosemary flavor), then remove the rosemary sprigs.

In a blender or food processor, puree the orange segments, rosemary leaves, rosemary-infused honey, heavy cream, and yogurt. Pour into ice pop molds until the mixture reaches ¼ inch from the top. Cover the molds and add ice pop sticks, per your mold's specifications. Freeze for at least 4 hours.

MAKE THE DRIZZLE

When the pops are frozen, melt the chocolate in a heatproof bowl nestled into a pot of boiling water. Stir in the oil and the salt, and whisk until fully combined.

GARNISH THE POPS

Line a baking sheet with parchment paper. Fill a small, widemouthed glass with chocolate drizzle. Set the salt, finely chopped rosemary, and orange zest nearby.

Remove the pops from their molds by running the molds under hot water while pulling upward on the sticks. Place the pops on the baking sheet, drizzle with chocolate (or dip for greater coverage), and sprinkle with the desired toppings. Return to the freezer. Let freeze for at least 10 minutes, then eat as desired!

Rosemary Eucalyptus Congestion Steam

This was a treatment I received any time I was sick with a cold as a child—a congestion-zapping elixir that doubled as a spa treatment and pore cleanser. Both rosemary and eucalyptus are deeply invigorating and astringent, busting through even the most stubborn mucus and opening nasal passages that might not have known they needed clearing.

This steam will awaken your mind, clarify your thoughts, and help move congestion through your body a bit more quickly. I find it to be deeply effective at jostling mucus stuck in the farther recesses of my lungs, the kind of mucus that's sticky and hard to express. Deep breaths of hot, humid air stimulate circulation and expand pores, improving tissues both inside and out. (Read: Get a facial while you cough up the junk in your lungs.)

nota bene: Steam is hotter than boiling water, so be very careful as you open and close the pot of steaming water. Also, the essential oil evaporates through rising steam, and eucalyptus oil can sting your eyes as it does so. Always close your eyes while inside your makeshift steam room.

The eucalyptus essential oil is completely optional, but it will intensify the congestion-busting effects.

for 1
preparation time: 7 minutes

Large pot (1 gallon or so) of water

10 large sprigs fresh rosemary, or more as desired

3 to 4 drops eucalyptus essential oil (optional), plus more as needed

Bath towel

Tissue to blow your nose

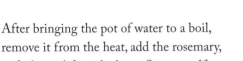

After bringing the pot of water to a boil, remove it from the heat, add the rosemary, and place a lid on the brew. Set yourself up at a counter or kitchen table with a comfortable stool or chair. Place the pot of water on a trivet or potholder to protect the surface below.

You'll use the towel to create a tent over your head and the pot of water, enclosing the steam.

With your bath towel and tissue close at hand, sit down in front of the pot and remove the lid. Add drops of eucalyptus oil, if using, and immediately cloak your head and the pot of water with the towel, closing your eyes. Breathe as deeply as you can. The moment you begin to feel too hot, come out from under the towel, put the lid back on the pot, and take a break.

Blow your nose. Repeat. Feel free to add more eucalyptus oil as it evaporates.

Breathe freely!

Coconut Rosemary Scalp Rub

I have always had a lot of hair (more on that later, when we make Lavender Sea Salt Beach Hair Spritz on page 186)—enough that it took me many decades to learn how to really groove with my mane. When I hit puberty and my locks transitioned from perfectly coiffable, always shiny child's hair to out-of-control frizzy teenage wave, nobody issued a memo to advise me I might want to put down my hairbrush. It was a long journey to the discovery that my hair behaved much better when it was left alone.

Yet leaving my hair alone also meant forgoing the regular scalp stimulation and cell renewal that came from hair brushing. I often went through phases of increased hair shedding, and I longed for a way to address this—aside from chalking it up to natural and inevitable hormonal vicissitudes.

I always knew that scalp massage felt like the touch of a thousand angels upon my body, but it wasn't until I asked my brilliant, homemade-hair-product-making hairstylist what he recommended, and he suggested rubbing my scalp with coconut oil, that I found my answer. Knowing that rosemary is said to stimulate follicle growth, I decided to infuse one into the other and spend some time giving my scalp the love it was crying out for.

Not only did it make a huge difference in my shedding, but I also found the process of giving myself a scalp rub at least once a week to be deeply relaxing. This is a self-care routine with a built-in stress buster. I love to do it at night before bed, as it helps relax me for sleep and allows the oil to soak in overnight before I wash it out (if necessary) the next morning.

makes 4 ounces
preparation time: 10 minutes + 2 to 4 hours infusion time

½ cup raw virgin coconut oil ┃ ¼ cup fresh rosemary leaves, washed and dried

In a medium saucepan, heat the oil over low heat. When it's hot, add the rosemary. Use a silicone spatula or wooden spoon to stir and massage the herbs against the base of the pan in order to release the oils. Keep over the heat for another 15 to 30 seconds, then remove from the heat. Cover the pan and let sit for 2 to 4 hours to infuse.

After this time, if the oil has hardened, return it to low heat to melt. Remove from the heat and strain through cheesecloth to separate and discard the rosemary leaves. Pour the infused oil into an airtight container and let cool completely; it's expected that the oil will return to at least a semi-solid state. Store in your bathroom, out of direct sunlight.

To use, scoop out about ½ teaspoon with your fingers and melt by rubbing between your fingertips. Apply directly to the scalp, using your fingertips to massage small circles over your entire skull, beginning at the base and working your way up to your forehead. Repeat as often as desired. If your hair becomes oily, simply wash and condition as usual.

7

SAGE

MY MOTHER WAS THE QUEEN OF RITUALS. She had a way of imbuing any moment with grace and significance, of writing a code of meaning into even the smallest occasion. Even standard holidays were innovated upon: We grew our own wheatgrass to fill Easter baskets, practiced gratitude rituals before leaving any place we'd stayed, and used each night of Chanukah as a moment for setting an intention of truth, peace, or other goodness that would permeate the year to come. She had an arsenal of ritual-creating devices always at the ready, including a pendulum for intuitive decision making, a healthy supply of rose quartz, a wide array of homeopathic remedies, and, of course, dried sage for burning.

Sage comes from the Latin *salvia*, which means to save, and while I cannot stand the smell of smudging sage (as it's called when burned in traditional indigenous American ritual practice), I learned early on to use the herb for the purposes of energetic clearing and renewal—its own kind of salvation. Today I prefer palo santo wood for smudging and like to keep sage in the realm of the kitchen.

As a cooking herb, sage possesses an elegance that elevates any dish to ritual status, suffusing savory and sweet flavors with an earthy sumptuousness.

Discover more of sage's properties on page 21.

Persimmon Bites with Pomegranate Molasses & Crispy Sage Leaves

Speaking of rituals, the first time I made these tender little bites was for a women's group I over-enthusiastically decided to spearhead in the year after my mother died. We each brought a passage to read about our relationship to creativity, and a dish to eat.

I was in awe of the intergenerational bridge we built that night, moved as much by what was shared as by the urgency of my own need to reinvent how I would be mothered in this new, motherless life. Love was all around, I just hadn't yet decided to let myself receive it.

And then, of course, there was the food. Kabocha squash stuffed with quinoa, feta, and herbs; salad bowls overflowing with homegrown greens and flowers; and hydrosol-infused kombuchas and juices. These women knew how to potluck. And, from me, these persimmon bites with pomegranate molasses and crispy sage. Though you might not imagine it on Maui, there is a gorgeous persimmon farm just miles from my childhood home, and we grew pomegranate in our front yard.

Perfectly passable and ideal for a crowd, these goat cheese–shmeared appetizers are especially nice for the holidays (or any occasion involving a lot of ladies and a fancy talking stick). When persimmons aren't available, try ripe pears of any variety in their place.

serves 4
preparation time: 10 minutes

CRISPY SAGE LEAVES

2 tablespoons olive oil

About 30 small fresh sage leaves

PERSIMMON BITES

2 ripe but not overly soft fuyu persimmons, sliced ¼ inch thick

2 ounces chèvre (goat cheese), at room temperature

¼ cup pomegranate arils

1 tablespoon pomegranate molasses or balsamic vinegar

Flaky sea salt, to taste

Freshly cracked black pepper, to taste

MAKE THE SAGE LEAVES

Heat the oil in a small frying pan. When the oil starts to sizzle, drop in the sage leaves and fry for 20 to 30 seconds. Remove the pan from the heat, and use a slotted spoon to take the sage leaves out of the oil. Set the leaves aside and reserve the oil.

MAKE THE PERSIMMON BITES

Spread each slice of persimmon with a shmear of cheese. Top with a sage leaf and a few pomegranate arils. Drizzle with the sage-infused oil and the pomegranate molasses. Finish with a pinch of salt and pepper.

Black Bean & Sage-Roasted Butternut Quesadillas

My earliest Mexican food memories are of a restaurant by the water in Tiburon, a point on the north coast of San Francisco Bay. The water lapped against the hulls of boats and the mellow, sunny scent of warm corn tortillas, black beans, and goat cheese was everywhere. That flavor palate will forever be at the heart of my Mexican food longings.

Those musings became exponentially more inspired when the vegan Mexican phenomenon that is Gracias Madre hit California. They first opened a few blocks from my apartment in San Francisco, and by the time I migrated south to LA, there was an outpost here, too (frequented by Beyoncé and Jay Z, according to my father and TMZ).

Though *vegan* and *Mexican food* are not three words you usually hope to hear in the same sentence, the food was transcendently delicious. My longtime favorite was the *quesadilla de camote*, an earthy blend of sweet potato, caramelized onion, cashew nacho cheese, and pumpkin seed salsa. Its subtle mix of sweet, savory, and spice inspired these equally nontraditional quesadillas.

Here, butternut squash meets sage and cumin on its way to pair with creamy black beans and goat cheese. These can easily be served vegan by omitting the goat cheese and sour cream. They'll be just as tasty, I promise.

serves 4 to 6
preparation time: 1 hour

SAGE-ROASTED BUTTERNUT PUREE

1 small butternut squash (about 1½ pounds)

3 tablespoons olive oil

20 fresh sage leaves, coarsely chopped

¾ teaspoon sea salt

2 pinches cayenne pepper

BLACK BEANS

1 tablespoon olive oil

1 garlic clove, crushed

1 teaspoon ground cumin

½ teaspoon ground coriander

1 (15-ounce) can black beans, rinsed and drained (about 1½ cups)

¼ teaspoon sea salt

QUESADILLAS

8 to 12 corn tortillas

2 ounces crumbled chèvre (goat cheese, about ½ cup), at room temperature

1 ripe avocado, sliced

Sour cream, to taste

Salsa (optional)

Hot sauce (optional)

MAKE THE PUREE

Preheat the oven to 450°F. Line a rimmed baking sheet with parchment paper. Peel the butternut squash, slice lengthwise, scoop out the seeds, and cut the squash into ¾-inch crescents. Place each crescent flat on the baking sheet. Drizzle with the oil and sprinkle on about two-thirds of the sage and ½ teaspoon of the salt. Roast for 20 to 25 minutes, or until tender and beginning to brown at the edges. Remove from the oven and puree in a food processor or blender with the remaining sage, the remaining ¼ teaspoon salt, and the cayenne until completely smooth. Set aside.

MAKE THE BLACK BEANS

Heat the oil in a frying pan over medium heat and add the garlic, cumin, and coriander. Sauté for a minute, until the garlic is fragrant, then add the beans and salt. Stir to incorporate the ingredients and use a fork to mash the beans, leaving some beans whole until you reach the desired texture. Reduce the heat to low and cover, continuing to cook for another 5 minutes. Remove from the heat and leave covered.

MAKE THE QUESADILLAS

Heat a 12-inch frying pan or cast-iron skillet over medium heat and warm 2 to 3 tortillas at a time, given the amount of space in the skillet. Once the tortillas are soft, pliable, and warm on both sides, shmear each one with a layer of butternut puree followed by a layer of the beans, followed by a crumble of cheese. Fold each tortilla and flip over, allowing the ingredients to warm in the pan. Cook for 1 to 2 minutes on each side, then serve immediately, with avocado, sour cream, salsa, and hot sauce, as desired.

Creamy Fresh Corn Polenta with Sage, Parmesan & Crispy Shallots

I don't like my kitchen creations to be fussy or overly complex, or to take an absurdly long time to make. Even though many of the recipes in this book are low and slow infusions, I like simple techniques with big payoff. To that end, I love a good bowl of mush. The more flavorful the mush the better—hence my love of blended soups, refried beans, and this dreamy, cheesy, richly textured polenta.

The poetry of serving corn in two forms is deeply fulfilling, and its sweetness is matched by the salty brine of Parmesan and the pungency of fried shallots. This is a bowl of food to be savored over and over again—and would be as delicious for breakfast or brunch (perhaps with an egg on top) as it is for lunch and dinner.

May it bring you as much comfort as it does me.

nota bene: Using a tip from *The Science of Good Cooking*, I discovered the anti-clumping magic of adding a pinch of baking soda to polenta. It's a gem.

serves 4
preparation time: 40 minutes

FRESH CORN POLENTA

7 cups water

½ cup heavy cream

1½ teaspoons sea salt, plus more to taste

Pinch of baking soda

1½ cups coarse cornmeal (polenta)

2 tablespoons minced fresh sage leaves, plus more for garnish

3½ ounces Parmesan cheese, grated (about 1 cup), plus more for garnish

2 cups fresh corn kernels (or frozen if fresh is unavailable), ¼ cup reserved for garnish

Freshly cracked black pepper, to taste

CRISPY SHALLOTS

¼ cup olive oil

¾ cup thinly sliced shallots

Flaky sea salt, to taste

MAKE THE POLENTA

Place the water and heavy cream in a large pot and bring to a boil. Add the salt and baking soda and stir to dissolve. Add the cornmeal in a constant stream, and bring back to a boil, stirring constantly. Turn the heat to the lowest setting and put a lid on the pot. Let cook for another 25 minutes.

MAKE THE SHALLOTS

Place the oil in a 12-inch frying pan over medium heat. After 1½ minutes or when the oil shimmers, test the heat by flicking a drop of water in the oil; when it sizzles, add the shallots with a couple of sprinkles of salt. Stir with a silicone spatula to ensure the shallots fry evenly. When they turn golden brown and the edges are browning (4 to 5 minutes), use a slotted spoon to place the shallots in a small bowl. Reserve the infused oil in the pan.

Once the polenta has cooked the additional 25 minutes, stir in 1 tablespoon of the infused oil, the sage, Parmesan, and 1¾ cups of the corn. Taste, and stir in additional salt as desired. Remove from the heat and let sit for 5 to 10 minutes to allow the flavors to meld. Stir in ¼ cup of the shallots. Serve topped with the ¼ cup corn, the remaining shallots, sage, and Parmesan. Finish with the cracked black pepper.

Sage Salted Caramel Ice Cream

Let's go back to that glorious moment when a friend and I were vegan donut shopping in the San Francisco Ferry Building, as self-respecting hipsters are wont to do on a weekend. As I selected donuts of kaffir lime and blackberry lavender, he called me out for liking my flavors to be scents. The truth is, I don't just want my flavors to be scents. I want them to be multidimensional sensory experiences. I want them to be food for all five senses. So when it came time to develop a requisite caramel for the book, I approached the recipe from as many sensory angles as I could.

Though a rosemary or floral caramel was tempting, I wanted something gutsier, rootsier, more elemental: I wanted sage.

The fusion of sage and caramel unites two flavors that take well to burning, to heat, to ingredients that morph from one state to the next with ease. Transformation is the gift of caramel—melting butter and sugar becoming transcendent confection—as much as it is the traditional, ritual power of sage.

This ice cream, spiked with salt and coconut sugar, is a multidimensional dessert fit for summoning spirits.

makes 1 quart
preparation time: overnight ice cream maker
freeze + 1 hour 20 minutes + 6 to 7 hours chill time

SAGE SALTED CARAMEL

1½ cups coconut sugar or granulated sugar

¼ cup water

½ cup heavy cream

½ teaspoon sea salt

20 fresh sage leaves

ICE CREAM BASE

2 egg yolks

2 cups heavy cream

1½ cups whole milk

¼ teaspoon vanilla seeds scraped from the pod, or ½ teaspoon pure vanilla extract

¼ teaspoon sea salt

About 60 fresh sage leaves

PREPARE YOUR ICE CREAM MAKER

The night before you plan to make the ice cream, freeze the bowl of your ice cream maker.

MAKE THE CARAMEL

These instructions are for coconut sugar. If you use cane sugar, the sugar may need to cook longer to reach a deep caramel color and flavor. In a medium saucepan over medium heat, stir the coconut sugar and water until the sugar dissolves. Raise the heat to medium-high and bring to a boil, swirling the contents of the pan without stirring. Continue to cook for another 1 to 2 minutes, being careful not to let the mixture burn. This coconut sugar caramel is unusual in that it doesn't need to cook long in order to reach a deep amber color and achieve a strong depth of taste. Once it's been at a simmer for 2 to 3 minutes total, remove from the heat and add the heavy cream and salt. Whisk to combine, and add the sage. Let the sage steep for about 25 minutes.

Strain out the sage leaves and let the caramel cool for at least 20 minutes.

MAKE THE ICE CREAM

Whisk the egg yolks in a medium bowl. In a large saucepan over medium heat, warm ¾ cup of the sage caramel (reserve the remaining caramel to top the ice cream) with the heavy cream, milk, vanilla, egg yolks, and salt, whisking until steam rises. Add the sage.

Cook over low heat, stirring continuously, for 20 to 25 minutes, until the temperature reaches 170°F, or until the custard thickens slightly and coats the back of a spoon. Taste to see if you've reached the desired level of sage-iness, and if so, strain out the sage leaves. If not, leave the sage leaves in to steep while the custard cools.

Transfer the custard to a bowl and cool completely in the fridge. Once chilled, if the sage is still in the custard, strain it out and discard. Freeze in an ice cream maker, according to the manufacturer's instructions, until the consistency is smooth and thick, then transfer to an airtight container and freeze for at least 6 hours before eating. Top with the reserved sage salted caramel.

No ice cream maker? The results won't be as refined, but follow the process on page 38.

Citrus Sage Tonic (Vegan)

I have never been very wild, at least not in the Cabo San Lucas–spring breakers sense of the word. My brand of wildness tends to manifest in quiet river skinny-dipping, or playing fast and loose in the kitchen, or not wearing pants all day, or singing to Beyoncé at the top of my lungs.

And yet, there is one touch of wild that's been with me from the time I first began drinking alcohol: I love tequila. The tequila that haunts so many is not my tequila; my tequila is a gentle beauty, full of laughter and sweetness and nary a hangover. I don't know how I got so lucky (perhaps it's just that I'm a true lightweight and drink only a touch at a time), but tequila has always been a friend to me. And to this Kale & Caramel riff on a traditional *paloma* cocktail.

While this tonic is absolute perfection sans tequila, I can joyfully recommend it with the liquor as well. And when you do choose to transition your tonic from morning sunshine to evening *olé*, know that I'm out here raising a glass to your (tender, intelligent) wildness.

serves 2 to 3

preparation time: 10 minutes

3 fresh sage leaves

1 to 2 tablespoons agave nectar, depending on the sweetness of the grapefruits

2 large grapefruits, juiced (about 2 cups)

1 lime, juiced (about 2 tablespoons)

1 large lemon, juiced (about ¼ cup)

Sea salt, to taste

Ice cubes, for serving

Use a muddler or a wooden spoon to crush the sage into the agave nectar at the bottom of a cocktail shaker. Add the grapefruit, lime, and lemon juices and a few pinches of salt. Shake vigorously, then strain out over ice.

MAKE IT A COCKTAIL!
Tequila, mezcal, gin, vodka.

8

THYME

I WAS IN THE SHOWER the first moment when death came and stood next to me. I had just moved home from Michigan, just found out that my mother was ill, that love was not as I imagined, that the bonds that held the world together in one piece were actually looser and far less cohesive than I had imagined.

I stood in the shower with my hair wet and streaming down my back, thick rivulets of water coursing down my temples, my hands making circles to clean the parts of my body that could be made, temporarily, anew. I thought about all the love I had felt in my life, all the hungry gulps of sex and affection and loyalty and friendship that I'd taken. All the moments of devotion between my mother and me.

And then, just as quickly as death had come, the world rushed in to chase it away, the water hot and beating down on my neck. I turned the shower handle and got out of the tub. I turned my back on death, but I knew, suddenly, that there was only one thing that mattered: to belong to myself, no matter what death would ask of me, no matter what it would take away.

Thyme, earthbound and serious, is also a shape-shifter. It dances on the boundary of savory and sweet, boasting more than four hundred varietals. A few of these varietals—English, French, lemon, mother-of-thyme, and several others—are appropriate for eating, delivering a woodsy, elemental flavor to anything they touch. Thyme's versatility makes it particularly thrilling in the kitchen, where it pairs as well with tangy feta and tomatoes as it does with honeycomb and nectarines. At the Kale & Caramel garden party, thyme shows up to add depth and pungent aroma whenever it is needed.

It is also an exceptionally hardy herb, growing year-round and standing up to even the strongest of flavors. It is the herb that reminds me I need only ever be myself, even in the face of total loss.

Discover more of thyme's properties on page 21.

Braised Radicchio, Nectarine & Burrata Flatbread

As I restored myself, cellularly and emotionally, in the wake of deep grief, the act of writing not only became therapeutic, it pumped a kind of spiritual oxygen into my lungs. I wrote to make sense of things, to answer questions that haunted me, to keep my heart awake to the possibility of new life. And amidst it all, writing to each other daily, my friend Janson and I discovered the magic of something we called Infinite Selves: A Memoir of Singularity in Plurality, or IS:AMOSIP for short.

IS:AMOSIP was (and still is) a rotating roster of stories that capture the core human struggles we both—we all—experience. The heartbreak, the loss, The Longing™, the absurd and hilarious difficulty of just being human. Somehow, knowing that my suffering was understood by this one other human—whose life was externally so different from my own, yet whose heart was so close to mine—provided the levity and verve I needed to keep writing my own story, a new story. A new memoir of singularity in plurality.

And so this flatbread was born, a memoir in food form, created by Janson and me the summer when I moved to Los Angeles. When we first made it, it was an experiment, a dish we both knew might sound more poetic than it tasted. But thyme made the poetry perfect, radicchio spelled out the bitterness of loss, and nectarines reminded us of the good in our blood. It was electric—a flatbread for sweetness, for telling new stories.

For memoirs of singularity in plurality.

makes 1 large or 2 smaller pizzas
preparation time: about 35 minutes + 3 to 4 hours
if making your own pizza dough

16 ounces pizza dough, store-bought or homemade (see page 119)

Cornmeal, for the pizza stone or baking sheet

1 medium head radicchio, thinly sliced

1 tablespoon plus 2 teaspoons olive oil

1 tablespoon balsamic vinegar, plus more for drizzling

1 tablespoon honey

¼ teaspoon flaky sea salt, plus more to taste

1 large shallot, thinly sliced

2 medium yellow nectarines or peaches, sliced ⅛ to ¼ inch thick

1 tablespoon fresh thyme leaves

8 ounces fresh burrata cheese

Truffle oil, optional (but highly recommended)

MAKE THE RADICCHIO

Set aside ⅓ cup of the radicchio to sprinkle atop your finished pizzas, and place the rest of the radicchio in a pan with the 1 tablespoon oil, the vinegar, honey, and the ¼ teaspoon salt. Cook on medium heat for 5 to 7 minutes, stirring occasionally, until things start getting caramely and deep brown and tender. In a separate pan over medium heat, sauté the shallot in the 2 teaspoons oil and a sprinkle of salt until it's slightly browned.

MAKE THE FLATBREAD

Preheat the oven to 475°F.

Sprinkle a large pizza stone or baking sheet with cornmeal and stretch 1 large ball or 2 smaller balls of dough by letting them hang from both hands until they reach the desired shape and evenness. The edges can be slightly thicker than the middle, and the whole thing should be quite thin, as it will rise. It's a pretty forgiving piece of dough, so don't worry too much.

Drizzle the dough with a generous hand of olive oil and a sprinkle of salt.

If making 2 pizzas: Spread half the braised radicchio atop one of the stretched-out pizza doughs, and sprinkle with half the shallot. Arrange half the nectarines on top. Sprinkle with the thyme, drizzle with vinegar (or balsamic glaze, if you happen to have it), and add some extra salt. Do the same on the second pizza. If making 1 pizza: Follow the same instructions, using all the ingredients at once.

Bake for 10 minutes. Remove and dollop with the burrata. Return to the oven for 3 to 5 minutes, or until the pizzas reach your desired level of crispy-edged brownness and cheesy bubbliness. Once you remove them from the oven, dress them with the reserved radicchio and drizzle with extra vinegar and the truffle oil, if you choose. Serve immediately.

Thyme-Scented Plum & Arugula Salad with Honey Hazelnut Clusters

Things with my father were not easy after my mother died. We were two utterly different humans walking—and often stumbling on—distinct paths of grief. My hurt was so deep, my longing so great, that no salve but time could make a difference. Time, and a willingness to get to know my father for who he was, instead of simply longing for my mother.

I began this process with a willful study of his unique person, the things he liked, the ways we might connect. In the same manner as I would have studied a stranger I hoped to call a friend, I sorted and sifted through my father's loves and hates, his history, his quirks. I wanted to see him without the pall of my mother hanging over him.

And after a time, things changed. I discovered I loved watching basketball with him, loved walking miles with him on the mountain highway above my childhood home, loved his wry and generous sense of humor. I guess, perhaps, we became friends.

This is the salad I made for him—lover of arugula that he is—the year I remember feeling that Father's Day could be a celebration once again. The pepper of arugula is mirrored in the honey hazelnut clusters, brightened by fresh plums, and mellowed with salty ricotta salata. Like any honest family, it's complex and feisty, but deeply satisfying.

serves 4
preparation time: 15 minutes

HONEY HAZELNUT CLUSTERS

⅓ cup toasted hazelnuts, coarsely chopped

2 teaspoons honey

¼ teaspoon sea salt

¼ teaspoon freshly cracked black pepper

BALSAMIC THYME VINAIGRETTE

1½ tablespoons olive oil

1½ tablespoons balsamic vinegar

¾ teaspoon honey

1½ tablespoons minced shallot

1½ teaspoons minced fresh lemon thyme leaves

¼ teaspoon sea salt, plus more to taste

Pinch of freshly cracked black pepper

PLUM AND ARUGULA SALAD

2 plums, washed, pitted, and sliced into sixths or eighths

1 teaspoon fresh thyme leaves

4 to 5 large handfuls baby arugula, washed and dried (about 5 ounces)

¼ cup thinly sliced ricotta salata or hemp seeds

MAKE THE HAZELNUT CLUSTERS

Preheat the oven to 450°F. In a small bowl, mix the hazelnuts, honey, salt, and pepper and stir to coat the nuts evenly. Spread in an even layer on a small rimmed baking sheet. Bake for 2 to 3 minutes, until bubbling and beginning to turn golden. Remove from the oven, push the nuts into small clusters, and set aside.

MAKE THE VINAIGRETTE

Whisk together all the ingredients and set aside.

MAKE THE SALAD

In a small bowl, toss the plum slices with the thyme. Let sit for 5 to 10 minutes to allow the herbs to flavor the fruit. Place the arugula in a salad bowl, add the plums, and toss with the vinaigrette. Top with the hazelnut clusters and ricotta salata.

Roasted Tomato Soup with Thyme-Crusted Grilled Cheese

Perhaps because I've reinvented myself in so many different parts of the country, in so many professions, and haircuts, and playlists, and boyfriends—or perhaps because I long for the comfort I imagine is embedded in the bond of siblings—my friendships have always been deeply important to me. Because I am an only child, my closest friends are the sibling confidants and conspirators I never had. And yet, finding such deep platonic connections changes as we grow older and less attuned to the gleeful and sublimely romantic pastime of new friendship.

Sometimes, though, a new friend comes into your life when you least expect it and, in a flash, you cannot imagine ever having lived without her. I met Kira by happenstance, while having lunch with a friend from college and her boss, who was Kira's mother. Kira popped by, and the four of us spent the next five hours drinking wine and sloshing through pizza, laughing our faces off, and finally, driving Kira home to get ready for a date with her then-boyfriend, now-husband.

At that point, Kira and I had already fallen a little bit in friend love. She was, all of a sudden, the sister I'd never had. Even today, Kira sends me cards (yes, real cards, in the mail) that say, "I love you. That's all."

Over the next few months, in the magic of our own early friendship, Kira and I connected with a group of four other women who all—miraculously—loved each other. Now, the group of us—spread out from India to Hawaii to Palo Alto to LA—makes a point to take vacations together, eat pizza together, cry together, grow together. There are months when it's hard, when our union does not hold together just right, and then, in seconds of togetherness, it all comes back—the way sisterhood holds a part of our hearts above everything else.

This is the meal Kira and I shared one fall evening when I was just starting Kale & Caramel— the meal that feels, to me, like the safety of someone you love holding your hand. For all of that, there is roasted tomato soup and cheddar-thyme grilled cheese.

serves 3 to 4
preparation time: 35 to 40 minutes

ROASTED TOMATO SOUP

½ cup sliced yellow onion

3 teaspoons fresh thyme leaves

1½ teaspoons sea salt

1 tablespoon plus 1 teaspoon olive oil

4 garlic cloves, coarsely chopped

¼ to ½ teaspoon ground black pepper, depending on how much of a kick you want

1 (28-ounce) can whole fire-roasted tomatoes (or regular canned tomatoes, if fire-roasted are unavailable)

1 cup vegetable broth

2 tablespoons plain yogurt

THYME-CRUSTED GRILLED CHEESE

2 tablespoons salted butter, at room temperature, plus more for the pan

2 teaspoons fresh thyme leaves

6 to 8 slices bread, depending on the number of sandwiches desired

1½ to 2 cups grated sharp cheddar cheese

MAKE THE SOUP

In a stockpot, sauté the onion, thyme, and salt in the oil over medium heat. Stir occasionally for 3 to 5 minutes, then add the garlic and ¼ teaspoon of the pepper. Sauté until the garlic becomes fragrant and the onion starts to soften, another 5 minutes or so. Continue to stir as you add the tomatoes and broth, and increase the heat to medium-high. Bring to a simmer, then cover with a lid, reduce the heat, and simmer for 10 minutes.

Remove from the heat and place the soup in a blender. Add the yogurt. Pulse or blend on high until the soup is creamy but still has a bit of texture. Pour back into the pot and keep warm until serving.

MAKE THE GRILLED CHEESE

In a small dish, cream the room-temperature butter with the thyme. Butter one side of each slice of bread, and top the unbuttered side of one slice with ⅓ to ½ cup cheese. Top with the other slice of buttered bread, buttered side up. Repeat as needed.

Butter a large frying pan and warm over medium-low heat for 2 minutes. Add the sandwiches and cover the pan, letting the sandwiches cook until the cheese begins to melt, 2 to 3 minutes. Uncover, press the sandwiches down with a spatula, and flip to the other side. Cook for another 2 to 3 minutes, until the cheese is entirely melted and the bread is golden brown.

Serve immediately, with the soup.

Fig & Honeyed Thyme Ricotta Galette

Figs, like no other fruit, send me into shamanic baking reveries. They speak to me, informing me of exact flavor and herb pairings, telling me precisely how they want to be eaten. Perhaps it's our history, the love I cultivated over so many years with the fig tree that grew outside my window as a child. Sometimes, not wanting to go out the back door through my parents' bedroom, I'd pour myself out the folding windows and run over grass and lava rock, just up the hill to where the fig's branches spread like honey over the land.

It was always a duel between the mynah birds and the humans for the lion's share of the fruit, and I was not one to lose. I wanted those soft, pale green orbs all for myself, wanted to break open their topaz flesh and actually, perhaps, become a fig myself. It didn't seem the worst lot in life.

Last summer, figs came to me whispering of being made into a galette, my most favorite of pastries. A galette with ricotta and thyme and honey and lemon zest, to be precise. The next day, I procured the necessary fruits and carted myself out to the home of friends in the wilds of Burbank, where I went into full-force galette mode.

We devoured it outside at sunset, by their pool, surrounded by lavender, jasmine, and backyard mint. It was everything the figs had whispered to me. The lemon zest and honey are ideal counterparts to the figs' earthiness and the thyme's complexity. The ricotta is subtly tart and smooth.

And now, I bestow upon you the keys to making figs your lover.

serves 6

preparation time: 1 hour 30 minutes

PASTRY CRUST

1¼ cups pastry flour, plus more for rolling

3 tablespoons granulated sugar

¼ teaspoon sea salt

8 tablespoons (1 stick) salted butter, chilled

2 to 3 tablespoons ice water

RICOTTA CUSTARD

1 egg

⅓ cup whole-milk ricotta

2½ teaspoons honey

2½ teaspoons granulated sugar

1 teaspoon lemon juice

½ teaspoon pure vanilla extract

½ teaspoon fresh thyme leaves

½ teaspoon lemon zest

FIG AND HONEYED THYME FILLING

4 to 5 large ripe figs, sliced to create ½-inch wedges

½ teaspoon fresh thyme leaves

½ teaspoon lemon zest

Honey, for drizzling

MAKE THE CRUST

At least 30 minutes in advance, mix the flour, sugar, and salt in a bowl. Cut the butter into small pieces (or grate it) and use a pastry cutter or fork to work it into the flour mixture until it's almost fully incorporated. Add 2 tablespoons of the ice water (you can add more later if need be) and work the dough for just a few moments more until it is smooth and cohesive. Add another ½ to 1 tablespoon ice water if the dough is too dry or crumbly. Form into a disk about ½ inch thick and cover in plastic wrap. Place in the fridge.

MAKE THE CUSTARD

Separate the egg yolk from the white, reserving the egg white in a bowl in the fridge to use on the crust later. Mix the egg yolk with ricotta, honey, sugar, lemon juice, vanilla, thyme, and lemon zest in a small bowl with a whisk or spoon until fully incorporated. Cover with plastic wrap and place in the fridge.

ASSEMBLE THE GALETTE

Preheat the oven to 400°F. When the dough has chilled for at least an hour, remove it from the fridge and lightly dust a piece of parchment paper with flour (the dough will stay on this parchment paper for baking, so it can be as big as the baking sheet you'll bake on). Begin to flatten the disk of dough by tapping its surface in a circle with the rolling pin—flattening it out as you go. Roll out to ¼ inch thick. Place the parchment paper and the rolled dough onto a baking sheet.

Spread the ricotta custard in a circle in the center of the dough, using the back of a spoon to distribute it evenly, leaving a 1½- to 2-inch perimeter of dough that will fold over the filling.

Arrange the fig slices in concentric(ish) circles starting in the center and filling in the space as you work your way out to the edge of the custard. Sprinkle with the thyme and lemon zest and drizzle with honey. Then fold in the edges of the dough, layering sections as you please. Make sure there are no tears or gaps (to prevent leaking).

Lightly beat the reserved egg white and brush it on the exposed dough. Bake for 35 to 40 minutes (checking at 30 to estimate the remaining time), until the top is golden brown and the bottom is starting to caramelize. Bask in the heavenly scent filling your house.

When it's done, let cool for 10 minutes before serving.

Lemon Thyme Vanilla Bean Sorbet

When I was young, I used to thrill at the thought of going over to my mother's best friend Jan's house. It meant pool time, and garden time, and the novelty of being girls together. Jan was surrounded by a family of boys, and my mom and I were glad to invite another woman into our coven of two. Watching Jan and my mom weave the magic they did in their homes, I learned the finer arts of hosting, of cooking, of decorating, of making beauty out of the entirely mundane.

With Jan, I first discovered the magic of a pungent lemon sweet, initially through her homemade lemon curd. Tart desserts are some of my favorites now, as they imbue as much flavor through scent as they do through taste itself.

When I first made this sorbet, I was astonished at the results—the vanilla bean, lemon thyme, and lemon juice commingle to produce a flavor that is rich and heady yet irrepressibly mouthwatering. It's incredibly tart; for a time, I worried it was too tart. But the truth was in the eating: I consumed nearly a quart of it by myself in the days after making it. I couldn't stop. I was drunk on mouth-puckering sorbet.

Yet for all its perfection, I wanted to add a balancing flavor and texture to the mix: Enter lemon-zested whipped cream, a luscious cloud upon which to experience the extreme tartness of the sorbet. They're the ideal match, one supporting the other, rather than either overpowering. With berries, suffused with the gentle earthiness of lemon thyme, it's a dream.

nota bene: This is an extremely tart sorbet. If it puts too much pucker in your pout when you taste the mixture pre-freeze, feel free to adjust the sweetness to your liking.

makes 1 quart
preparation time: overnight ice cream maker
freeze + 25 minutes + 6 hours chill time

LEMON THYME VANILLA BEAN SORBET

¾ cup plus 2 tablespoons honey, or more to taste

1½ cups water

1¼ cups fresh lemon juice

½ teaspoon vanilla seeds scraped from the pod, or 1 teaspoon pure vanilla extract

Pinch of sea salt

10 to 12 sprigs fresh lemon thyme or regular thyme, washed and dried

LEMON-ZESTED WHIPPED CREAM

(this is enough for 3 to 4 people; expand the batch accordingly if more is needed)

½ cup chilled heavy cream

1 tablespoon honey or pure maple syrup

1 teaspoon lemon zest

GARNISH

Fresh berries

PREPARE YOUR ICE CREAM MAKER

The night before you plan to make the sorbet, freeze the bowl of your ice cream maker.

MAKE THE SORBET

Heat the honey, water, lemon juice, vanilla, and salt over medium heat, whisking just until the mixture begins to simmer. Remove from the heat. Slightly crush the thyme sprigs and immerse them in the honey mixture to allow the leaves to release their oils. Cover the pot and let steep for 30 minutes.

Remove the thyme and discard. Chill completely in the fridge. Once chilled, taste and adjust the sweetness as desired. Freeze the mixture in an ice cream maker, according to the manufacturer's instructions, until the consistency is smooth and thick, then transfer to an airtight container and freeze for at least 6 hours before eating.

No ice cream maker? The results won't be as refined, but follow the process on page 38.

MAKE THE WHIPPED CREAM

In a large bowl, use an electric hand mixer to whip the heavy cream, honey, and lemon zest until soft peaks form.

Serve the sorbet with fresh berries and lemon-zested whipped cream.

Pomegranate & Thyme
Spritzer (Vegan)

Every day, at sunset, my father marches out onto his front porch, sits with sunglasses and various reading material close at hand, and sips a drink as the sun settles itself into the wide blue swath of horizon straight ahead. Preferably, this sunset drink ritual is accompanied by a blasting of his favorite jazz of the moment—the dude truly knows how to get groovy. Growing up, my friends lovingly called him Martino Diamondé. He's just that kind of cool.

When I'm visiting, he calls me out to sit with him and Susan for the sunset as often as he can. It's his moment of true connection with the land, a land he's tended for decades. He understands the depth of preciousness he cares for: This land was, in the days of the Hawaiian monarchy, home to forests of sandalwood trees. Though sandalwood gave way to postcolonial ranches and vineyards, the 'āina—"land," in Hawaiian—remains sacred.

Hawaii's state motto—*ua mau ke ea o ka 'āina i ka pono*, "may the life of the land be perpetuated in righteousness"—reverberates everywhere. In my father. In me. It reminds me that we are still learning how to live with this earth, how to nurture it, how to grow with it. My father's daily sunset meditations are an umbilical cord to all of that—his way of rooting down, plugging in, being with the land.

My father's drink of choice used to be a martini—splash of vermouth, on the rocks, very dirty, with extra olives—but as he rounded into the sweetness of his late seventies, he's turned to less alcoholic beverages. So there is this, a rootsy spritzer that could transition seamlessly into a cocktail, were one inclined the Martino Diamondé way.

For sunsets and sacredness and remembering our umbilical connection to the earth.

serves 2

preparation time: 7 minutes

10 ounces pomegranate juice

1 teaspoon honey or sweetener of choice,
   to taste

1 teaspoon fresh lemon juice

1 teaspoon fresh thyme leaves

8 ounces sparkling water

Ice cubes, for serving

Fresh thyme sprigs, for garnish

Pomegranate arils, for garnish

2 to 3 twists freshly cracked black pepper
   (about ⅛ teaspoon)

Place the pomegranate juice, honey, lemon juice, and thyme in a blender and blend until fully incorporated.

   Pour equal amounts into 2 glasses and top with sparkling water. Add ice, as desired, and garnish with sprigs of thyme, pomegranate arils, and black pepper.

MAKE IT A COCKTAIL!

Vodka, gin, champagne, prosecco.

FLOWERS

I TEND TO REMEMBER THINGS SCENTUALLY, in aromatic mosaics of place, color, texture, and relationship. My deepest connection to my first human relationship—with my mother—was through scent. When I smelled her, I felt connected, rooted, and firmly placed in the world.

Though she never wore perfume, she was constantly surrounded by essential oils. Distillations of rose, clary sage, juniper, rosewood, frangipani, and lavender were my childhood friends. My mother taught me their properties, and I grew up immersed in the cosmology of scent, taking in by osmosis a healing modality that sprang from, and linked me back to, the natural world.

Today, this connection with plants and flowers supports balance on mental, physical, and spiritual planes. Rose lifts a heavy heart. Jasmine soothes a frenzied mind. Lavender helps me breathe more easily.

Each chapter that follows explores flowers I use in my everyday life, whether in their whole or distilled form, constellation points forming a map of joy. Many of these recipes are body and beauty products: There is something undeniably gratifying and comforting about using products on my body that are also edible. Beyond the obvious sensuality of slathering myself with honey and coconut oil, I find it deeply soothing to know that everything I'm putting on my skin is pure enough to eat.

In a world where we're continually bombarded by over-processed and chemically enhanced food, beauty, and home products, these plant-based concoctions are a much-needed reprieve. Your body will thank you.

FLOWER STORAGE

Treat fresh edible flowers with the same care you would a bouquet of flowers—minus any chemical-laden floral preservatives. Trim the stems and any unwanted leaves, and keep in a vase, jar, or glass filled with water, and out of the sun. Do not pluck blossoms or petals from the flower until just before you need them, as they will wilt quickly.

SOURCING LAVENDER

Fresh and dried edible lavender can often be found in bulk at co-ops and health food stores, at farmers' markets, and online. Make sure that you use only organic or homegrown lavender that has not been exposed to pesticides.

SOURCING JASMINE

While fresh, edible jasmine can be found in abundance during spring months (make sure you pick unsprayed, edible varietals), most of these recipes call for jasmine in green tea form, available at any grocery store.

SOURCING ROSE AND ORANGE BLOSSOM

You'll find dried edible rose petals in bulk at co-ops and health food stores, and online. Rose water and orange blossom water can be sourced at most grocery stores, in either the baking or international foods aisles.

I also suggest starting an in-home apothecary kit of essential oils. The oils I like to keep close are lavender, rose, rose geranium, jasmine, orange blossom, peppermint, eucalyptus, and tea tree. Essential oils can be found at many natural foods grocery stores, apothecary shops, and online; buy organic, therapeutic, or food grade whenever possible.

LAVENDER

FLAVOR PROFILE: European

FLORAL QUALITIES: Anxiety taming, depression lifting, sleep inducing

SAVORY FLAVOR PAIRINGS: Thyme, oregano, rosemary, lettuces, citrus, vinegar, root vegetables, cheese

SWEET FLAVOR PAIRINGS: Honey, vanilla, yogurt, oatmeal, goat cheese, citrus, blueberries, butter, caramel

JASMINE

FLAVOR PROFILE: European, Asian

FLORAL QUALITIES: Aphrodisiac, mood boosting, hormone regulating

SWEET FLAVOR PAIRINGS: Tea, chocolate, cream, honey, citrus

ROSE

FLAVOR PROFILE: European, Middle Eastern, Indian

FLORAL QUALITIES: Heart healing, compassion inducing, mind soothing

SAVORY FLAVOR PAIRINGS: Cumin, cardamom, root vegetables, cauliflower, vinegar

SWEET FLAVOR PAIRINGS: Honey, cardamom, pistachio, amaranth, watermelon, citrus, berries, yogurt, vanilla, caramel, butter, chocolate, stone fruit

ORANGE BLOSSOM

FLAVOR PROFILE: European, Middle Eastern, Indian

FLORAL QUALITIES: Aphrodisiac, anxiety relieving

SAVORY FLAVOR PAIRINGS: Root vegetables, nuts, citrus, olive oil, black pepper, chili

SWEET FLAVOR PAIRINGS: Honey, cinnamon, citrus, stone fruit, figs, cardamom, berries

9

LAVENDER

WHEN I WAS ELEVEN, I came home from school one day to find my mother in stern-jawed concentration over a number of essential oil bottles laid out on our breakfast counter. She was counting drops of lavender and sandalwood, measuring ounces of sweet almond oil and vitamin E. As suddenly as motherhood had come to her, she decided to return to her other element, formulating with the flowers.

It was long before aromatherapy hit the mainstream, but the flowers—and lavender in particular—were my mother's true and great love. Over the next decade, she and my father built an empire out of her adoration of—and expertise in—plants and blooms.

Together, my parents taught me what it meant to be an entrepreneur—the long hours, the dogged insistence on gradual and constant growth, the near impossibility of separating work and personal life. I learned what they had to sacrifice to grow, for themselves and for our family—and because they believed in bettering the way that people took care of themselves.

And lavender, lavender was always there: on her hands, in her hair, diffused into the air we breathed, in the bottles that shipped out across the world.

Lavender is an herbal panacea, known for taming burns, killing germs, soothing sleeplessness, reducing fever, battling anxiety, and instilling a feeling of calm. It's also an ideal floral accent to the buttery sweetness of caramel and honey, the brightness of citrus, and the tang of vinegar and other savory flavors.

Discover more of lavender's properties on page 171.

Butter Lettuce with Herbes de Provence Vinaigrette (Vegan)

The days stretch out like stones in the hot sun, lazy, heavy, punctuated only by water and the sun's relentless coming up and going down. We are in Palm Springs. We are making our own rituals. We have done this for almost five years now, come to celebrate the new year, the leaving behind of one self and the welcoming of another. Come to be made clean by the desert. We skinny-dip and make bountiful meals and go to bed full of the heat of the day and the laughter that comes in waves with the silence. On our first trip, we imagined future years when we'd be together there again, communally making ourselves anew, basking in the miracle of the California winter. And we did. And it only grew sweeter.

And then there was the food. At night, I'd often find a dog-eared copy of Ottolenghi's *Plenty* by my bed—a goodnight story from my friend Micah that was also a prelude to what we'd make the next day. On this past year's Palm Springs pilgrimage, we sat down to an exquisite New Year's Eve spread, thirteen of us come together to love and dance and talk about the beauty and the roughness that had made the year and would usher in the next.

We started with a salad that sang through my palate. I turned to Micah and whispered, "Is there lavender in this?" "Herbes de Provence," he confessed, "in the vinaigrette." And that was that—I knew I had to bring it to you.

This supremely simple salad will serve you well with just about any dish, as will the DIY herbes de Provence, which are delicious on cooked vegetable dishes, and anywhere else you fancy a sprinkle. The batch you'll be making is large enough to use on other roasted veggies, toasts, cheeses, and savory delights of your liking.

serves 4

preparation time: 10 to 15 minutes

HERBES DE PROVENCE MIX

3 tablespoons dried edible lavender buds

1 teaspoon dried thyme

1 teaspoon dried oregano

1 teaspoon dried rosemary

1 teaspoon fennel seeds

HERBES DE PROVENCE VINAIGRETTE

¼ cup olive oil

3 tablespoons red wine vinegar

1 tablespoon minced shallot

1 teaspoon herbes de Provence (store-bought or made with recipe at left)

½ teaspoon sea salt

SALAD

1 medium-large head butter lettuce, leaves washed and torn (about 8 cups loosely packed leaves)

MAKE THE HERBES DE PROVENCE

Mix the lavender, thyme, oregano, rosemary, and fennel seeds, and store in an airtight container out of the sun. If you want a finer blend, process the ingredients in a spice grinder or mortar and pestle until the desired texture is reached.

MAKE THE VINAIGRETTE

Place the oil, vinegar, shallot, herbes de Provence, and salt in a jar, seal with the lid, and shake vigorously, or whisk the ingredients in a small bowl.

SERVE THE SALAD

Place the lettuce in a salad bowl and toss with the vinaigrette. Serve immediately.

Mini Lavender Blueberry No-Bake Goat Cheesecakes

I remember best by smell and feel. The spicy, pungent roundness the afternoon sun drew out of our thick old carpeting, the smoothness of my mother's tan calves, the heat of our bodies. How we could be two bodies that felt like one. How most of her smelled like lavender and whatever she had picked in the garden just then, but her lap smelled only one way, all the time. When I was young and then again when I was a little older, I laid my head in her lap and smelled her singular aroma. I memorized her.

I traced my life from and to that point of olfactory comfort in the center of my mother's body, the place where my life began, and where hers began to end.

To celebrate my beginning, my mother made berry mandala cheesecakes for every birthday. So, for her, my first home, I created these mini blueberry lavender cheesecakes.

These are much easier than your traditional cheesecake—you don't even need an oven to make them. The goat cheese provides an airy tang without being overpowering, and lavender steeped into blueberry sauce is glorious. There's even an extra flair of lavender ground into the graham cracker crust. It's almost as good as your mom smelled when you were little.

makes 6 small jars (I use 7-ounce jars)
preparation time: about 50 minutes

LAVENDER GRAHAM CRACKER CRUST

9 graham crackers (1 sleeve)

½ teaspoon dried edible lavender buds, coarsely ground

Pinch of sea salt

4 tablespoons (½ stick) salted butter, melted

LAVENDER BLUEBERRY SAUCE

1½ cups fresh blueberries

¼ cup water

3 tablespoons granulated sugar

½ teaspoon Meyer lemon zest

¼ teaspoon pure vanilla extract, or ⅛ teaspoon vanilla seeds scraped from the pod

Pinch of sea salt

¾ teaspoon dried edible lavender buds

GOAT CHEESECAKE FILLING

¾ cup heavy cream, chilled

8 ounces cream cheese, at room temperature

4 ounces chèvre (goat cheese), at room temperature

½ cup granulated sugar

2 teaspoons lemon zest

½ teaspoon dried edible lavender buds, coarsely ground

CHEESECAKE TOPPINGS

Lemon zest

Dried edible lavender buds

MAKE THE CRUST

Break the graham crackers into pieces and place in a food processor. Process until they're a sandy texture, but not floury. Small bits remaining are fine. Transfer to a medium bowl. Toss with the lavender and pinch of salt. Pour the butter over the crumbs and use a spoon to integrate.

Press 3 to 4 spoonfuls in each of 6 small jars, pressing down and about ½ inch up the sides of the jar to compress the crumbs. Place in the freezer while you make the rest of the cheesecake.

MAKE THE SAUCE

Place the blueberries and the water in a food processor and blend until they're mostly homogenized, with some texture remaining. Empty the mixture into a small saucepan. Add the sugar, lemon zest, vanilla, and salt. Bring to a simmer over medium heat, stirring continuously.

Place the lavender in a reusable tea bag or cheesecloth pouch, seal, and add to the sauce. Reduce the heat and continue to stir as the lavender steeps. When the sauce has thickened,

about 10 minutes, remove from the heat. Continue to steep the lavender for another 15 to 20 minutes. Then remove the tea bag or pouch, squeeze out all the sauce, and discard the lavender. Let the sauce cool completely.

MAKE THE FILLING

In a large bowl, whip the heavy cream with an electric mixer until soft peaks form.

In a second large bowl, use the mixer to whip the cream cheese, goat cheese, sugar, lemon zest, and lavender. Once the mixture is fully combined, use a spatula to gently fold in the whipped cream.

ASSEMBLE THE CHEESECAKES

Pull the jars lined with graham cracker crust from the freezer. Place 2 to 3 spoonfuls of the lavender blueberry sauce in the base, then follow with 2 to 3 heaping spoonfuls of the cheesecake filling. Add another spoonful or two of sauce, then add more cheesecake filling. Top with a swirl of sauce, a bit of lemon zest, and a few lavender buds.

Refrigerate for at least 2 hours, then serve.

Honey Lavender Ice Cream with Lemon Curd Swirl

I can't stand fussy food. I want food to be good, to be wholesome, to be real, to make me want to jump up and down and cozy up with it and dance with it. No small portions or unintelligible ingredients, please. I want food I can eat with my hands, straight from the garden, naked and wild and fulfilling. Including my flowers.

Perhaps you won't be eating this ice cream with your hands (though don't let me stop you), but the experience of making and eating it can be just as elemental. While some may feel that floral flavors are overly precious, I disagree: Cooking with flowers is about as rootsy as it gets. It's a perfect barometer for the seasons, and a way to get even closer to the earth that is nourishing you every damn day of your life.

So, this ice cream: inspired by hot October afternoons in line for Bi-Rite Creamery in San Francisco, laced with a tangy sunshine stream of Meyer lemon curd. Meyer lemons have a particularly floral perfume that adds dimension to the lavender, but they can easily be subbed for your garden-variety lemon with no loss of magic.

This is a dessert to snack on, to spoon midmorning, to feast on after dinner in midsummer warmth, to reclaim fussy food as elemental.

makes 1 quart ice cream
preparation time: overnight ice cream maker
freeze + 1 hour 15 minutes + 7 to 8 hours chill time

LEMON CURD

2 to 3 large Meyer or regular lemons, zested and juiced (about ½ cup juice)

3 egg yolks

½ cup honey

⅓ cup granulated sugar

4 tablespoons (½ stick) unsalted butter, cut into 1-tablespoon pieces

Pinch of sea salt

ICE CREAM BASE

2½ cups heavy cream

1½ cups whole milk

½ cup honey

3 tablespoons dried edible lavender buds, plus more for garnish

2 egg yolks

PREPARE YOUR ICE CREAM MAKER

The night before you plan to make the ice cream, freeze the bowl of your ice cream maker.

MAKE THE LEMON CURD

You're going to make the lemon curd over a double boiler, so find a heatproof bowl that can nestle into a small or medium saucepan. Fill the saucepan with 2 to 3 inches of water (should not touch the bottom of the bowl) and bring to a boil, without the bowl on top. Reduce to a simmer.

In the heatproof bowl, whisk the lemon zest and juice, egg yolks, honey, and sugar. Set atop the simmering water and whisk continuously until the curd thickens slightly, 30 to 35 minutes. Remove from the heat and whisk in the pieces of butter one by one, letting each melt before adding the next. Stir in the salt. Let cool completely. Given the use of honey, the color will be a darker yellow, and the curd will thicken once it's cooled.

MAKE THE ICE CREAM

In a saucepan over medium heat, whisk the heavy cream, milk, and honey until steam rises. Place the lavender in a reusable tea bag or cheesecloth pouch, seal, and immerse it in the liquid to steep. Cover the pan, remove from the heat, and let steep for 25 minutes,

then squeeze the sachet to release the flavor, and remove.

In a small bowl, whisk the egg yolks with ½ cup of the ice cream mixture, then gradually whisk the egg yolk mixture back into the pan. Return to the stove, and cook over low heat, stirring continuously, until the custard reaches 170°F, 20 to 25 minutes, or until it thickens slightly and coats the back of a spoon.

Cool completely in the fridge. Freeze in the ice cream maker, according to the manufacturer's instructions, until the consistency is smooth and thick.

No ice cream maker? The results won't be as refined, but follow the process on page 38.

MAKE THE ICE CREAM AND LEMON CURD SWIRL

Place half the ice cream mixture in the base of a freezer-safe container, and drizzle over ½ cup of the lemon curd, using a knife or chopstick to swirl and marble it. Top with the remaining ice cream, and swirl the top with another ¼ cup curd. Sprinkle with the lavender. Cover and freeze for at least 6 hours before eating.

Store extra lemon curd in an airtight container in the fridge, to eat on toast, yogurt, or other treats.

Lavender Honey Lemonade

When I was young, my mother doused us both liberally with lavender, when I was sick, when we traveled, when I had bad dreams: It's the singular scent that most invokes the memory of motherly caretaking in my mind. But as much as lavender helped me heal numerous ailments, its mellow waft made me overwhelmingly melancholy after my mother died. I turned to other scents and memories, waiting for the moment when lavender's aroma would not sting my heart.

My return to lavender has been gradual, a subtle reckoning with memory and a reclaiming of a remedy as my own. In the alchemy of time, scents and flavors recovered their initial meaning, unwinding the trauma they took on in loss and grief. Lavender, eventually, became a tonic for ease once again. Tasting it, smelling it, drinking it, I was stronger knowing it held the specific healing powers my mother once taught me.

Now, lavender is a reminder of sweet grace on street corners, of the beauty that can thrive in the heat of an urban summer, of transformation through scent and memory. So, while lavender is elegant in taste and potent in herbal qualities, it is for me an avenue of individuation—a route to becoming the healer that once healed me. In liquid form, it's the perfect refresher on a hot summer day or a mellow spring morning. Drink and feel vitality, possibility, ease.

serves 2 to 4

preparation time: 15 to 20 minutes

2 teaspoons dried edible lavender buds

4 cups water

**2 large lemons, juiced (about ¼ cup plus
2 tablespoons juice)**

**5 to 6 tablespoons honey or sweetener of choice,
or to taste**

Ice cubes, for serving

Place the lavender buds in a reusable or
disposable tea bag or cheesecloth pouch
and seal. Bring the water to a boil. Add
the sealed bag of lavender. Steep for 10 to
15 minutes, then remove the sachet. Cool
completely.

Combine the lemon juice, chilled lavender water, and honey. The steeped lavender
water will turn an extraordinary shade of
pink! Stir or shake to combine, and serve
over ice.

MAKE IT A COCKTAIL!
Vodka, St. Germain, gin.

Lavender Sea Salt Beach Hair Spritz

My hair has always been a prominent feature: thick, red, and, from the time I was a teen, perpetually on the verge of an unruly, curly mass that felt epically beyond my control. It took me until my twenties to figure out that the secret to having luscious and tamable locks was much simpler than I'd ever imagined. On a trip home to Maui one year, I realized that my hair always looked best air-dried after an ocean swim. I knew of saltwater or "beach hair" sprays on the market, and I also knew that I could make one ten times better at home, for about one-twentieth the cost (no joke).

This beach hair spritz has the curl-making power of sea salt, the moisture and shine of sweet almond oil, and the mellow scent of lavender. It's my everything. I use it after each shampoo and conditioning to produce perfect waves and soft curls, and to perfume my locks with radiant scent.
   Buy yourself an empty spray bottle and start concocting. You're welcome.

makes 8 ounces
preparation time: 5 minutes

1 cup minus 1 tablespoon water

1 teaspoon pure sea salt (not chemically treated, bleached, or iodized)

1 teaspoon Night Night Oil (page 190), or 2 drops lavender essential oil plus 1 teaspoon sweet almond oil

Pour the water, salt, Night Night Oil, or the almond oil and lavender essential oil into a spray bottle. Screw on the spray top, and shake vigorously (50 to 100 shakes) to homogenize the ingredients.

Lavender is antibacterial and will help keep this spray from getting cooties over time, but do keep it in a cool place. Spray liberally on damp hair after a shower, prior to styling, or on dry hair for a follicle pick-me-up.

Lavender Oat Milk Bath

I spent so much of my childhood longing for stimuli and distraction and friendship and play that, as I grew older, I didn't realize how deeply I also needed quiet. Stillness, calm, silence, breath—all these were components of sanity as important as the constant connection I imagined I wanted. Deep rejuvenation and quiet were all imperative in order to grow.

Particularly as I began working as a business owner with a never-ending to-do list of growth checkpoints and daily duties, I realized I had to pay much closer attention to how I cared for my body and mind.

On a practical level, that meant asking for help—and accepting it from angels like my friend Jennie, who spent hours with me in my first holiday rush of packaging and shipping client gifts. Her kind hands, and the support of others, reminded me to be gentle with myself even as I was forging ahead in fierce boss lady style. I needed so very many touches of tenderness not to burn out.

And on a subtler level, I needed to carve out time to recharge with rituals that brought me ease and rejuvenation. Like lavender oat milk bathtime.

Here, oats and lavender ground into flour become a silky, fragrant bathtime ritual for spirit restoring and skin luxuriating. This milk bath can be made with any dried flower or herb of your choosing (other favorites include rose and rosemary).

makes enough for 1 to 2 baths
preparation time: 5 minutes

1 cup rolled oats

½ cup dried lavender buds

Combine the oats and lavender buds in a blender or spice grinder, and blend on high until they've become a flour. Add ¾ cup or more to a bath for a delightfully milky, skin-softening, nervous system-soothing experience.

Night Night Oil

The older I get, the more I find myself tethered to rituals of self-care that keep me sane, that help keep The Longing™ at bay. On a practical level, this means my post-shower routine has gotten longer and more involved, as I apply various shea butters, coconut balms, comfrey salves, scalp rubs, scar ointments, body oils, skin toners, and hair conditioners. On a more subtle level, this means that I spend time each night tending to my inner world before I go to sleep, often with the help of this lavender-infused oil.

Lavender has a calming, soothing effect on the nervous system, and I use its scent as the jumping off point for a ritual of clearing and nurturing. Oils can be anointing agents, a practice that's been around for millennia—anointing is a way of summoning all that is good and making room for old and repetitive thoughts, emotions, and spirits to depart.

Anointing my forehead and the back of my neck as I lie in bed before sleep, breathing in the tender scent of a flower made for thriving in clear blue summer light, I am renewed. Make your own. Anoint. Leave the longing behind.

Be your own messiah.

8 ounces sweet almond oil	½ cup dried lavender buds, or 4 drops lavender essential oil

IF USING DRIED LAVENDER

Heat the almond oil in a small saucepan over low heat, stirring continuously, until it is very hot but no bubbles form. Do not let it boil or simmer. Add the lavender buds and continue to stir, using a wooden spoon to gently massage the buds into the oil. Remove from the heat and let cool completely. Pour into a jar and seal.

Let the mixture sit overnight. Strain through cheesecloth or a reusable tea bag and pour the oil back into the jar. Seal and keep in a cool place, out of sunlight.

IF USING LAVENDER ESSENTIAL OIL

Pour the almond oil into a clean 8-ounce glass bottle and add the essential oil. Seal and shake 50 to 100 times to incorporate. Keep in a cool place, out of sunlight. Use as a face and body moisturizer and anointing oil.

For anointing, place on pulse points of the wrists, sides and back of the neck, and over the heart.

10

JASMINE

NO MATTER WHERE I AM, jasmine will always mean falling in love. I've fallen in love in every season: Over the phone in Maui's perpetual summer, with light and shadow playing through the leaves of the eucalyptus. In fall, with amber light angling through broad oak, in lines of poetry emailed hungrily across the continent. In winter, shoveling snow and trudging through ice and having the kind of sex only young people in winter have, proving their aliveness against the curse of cold. In the spring, in San Francisco, with jasmine drenching every block, a profusion of scent so potent I smelled it before I saw it.

And then again: Jasmine in New York, captured in a perfume I still wear, a fragrance that makes me want to make out with myself whenever I put it on.

And again: Jasmine plucked beachside on Maui after we watched the sky turn crystalline with stars, jasmine that I carried into his car as he drove fast, too fast, speeding away from me even as I sat next to him.

Again: Jasmine woven into flowers he arranged for me, giddy with infatuation until I realized the bouquet had been for another me, first, and they lost their scent.

And again: Night-blooming jasmine heavy in the humid air as we undressed in moonlight, under the papaya trees, mosquitoes eating us as voraciously as we consumed each other.

Jasmine. Love. Falling.

So of course jasmine is, for me, the height of poetry in scent and in food and in every potion I put on my body. I want a riot of jasmine everywhere I go.

nota bene: Many types of jasmine are toxic. The jasmine I use here is either dried with green tea, or fresh, of the *jasminum polyanthum* varietal (pink jasmine, common throughout the United States).

Discover more of jasmine's properties on page 171.

Matcha Coconut Cream Parfaits with Jasmine Shortbread (Vegan)

I can't stand not to talk about sex.

I feel suffocated by people who would prefer not to discuss their last orgasm or the weird places they've had sex or the crazy things they've dreamed about while not having sex. I confessed, somewhat sheepishly, to my equally psychosexually curious friend Brooke, that I don't like not being able to imagine what my friends are like in the wide-open vulnerability of the act. I'm by no means sex obsessed—in fact, I once went three years without having sex at all (highly unrecommended, for the record)—but I do find something elementally revealing about it, both the sex and the talking about it. I cannot hide from myself in sex, nor can my partner hide from himself.

At its best, sex opens portals for previously unexplored avenues of connection. And at its worst—well, honestly I prefer not to have bad sex, so I'll leave it at that.

Parfaits are individually portioned riffs on trifle, and trifle will, for me, always mean sex. It's a sexy food, with gemstones of fruit and cream and cake, layers upon layers of sweetness and texture and tang and wild. It's a great food to make with and for and before and after sex. This is a vegan, cookie-studded version, infused with chlorophyll-rich, life-giving matcha, and the intoxicating scent of jasmine.

Eat it in spring, when the birds and bees are teaching the rest of us how to be. Or in winter, for that matter, when our need to remember our bodies is stronger than ever.

makes about six 1-cup parfaits
preparation time: about 1 hour

JASMINE SHORTBREAD

¼ cup plus 2 tablespoons loose-leaf jasmine green tea (or taken from jasmine tea bags)

2 cups all-purpose flour

½ teaspoon sea salt

1 cup plus 1 tablespoon raw virgin coconut oil, solid but scoopable

¾ cup confectioners' sugar

MATCHA COCONUT CREAM

2 (13.5-ounce) cans full-fat coconut milk, refrigerated upside down

1 tablespoon plus 1 teaspoon matcha tea powder

1 teaspoon pure vanilla extract, or ½ teaspoon vanilla seeds scraped from the pod

2 teaspoons lemon zest

¼ cup confectioners' sugar

PARFAIT TOPPINGS

Fresh berries

Lemon zest

MAKE THE SHORTBREAD

Preheat the oven to 325°F. Grind the jasmine tea in a (clean) spice or coffee grinder until it's a fine powder. In a medium bowl, whisk the ground tea with the flour and salt. In a second medium bowl, cream the oil and sugar until no clumps remain. Switch to a silicone spatula and fold in the dry ingredients, mixing to form a cohesive dough. Knead for 1 to 2 minutes: As the oil softens under the warmth of your hands, the dough will become more pliant and cohesive. Flatten into a 1-inch-thick disk.

Line a baking sheet with parchment paper and place the dough disk in the center. Use a rolling pin to roll the dough into a ½-inch-thick rectangle. Refrigerate for 10 to 15 minutes. Once the dough is firm, slice it into 2- to 3-inch shortbread fingers, about ¾ inch in width. Spread out evenly on the baking sheet. Bake for 20 to 25 minutes, until light golden brown. Let cool completely.

MAKE THE CREAM

Open the bottom (yes, the bottom) of each can of chilled coconut milk and scoop out the thick coconut cream, discarding the rest of the liquid. In a large bowl, mix the coconut cream with the matcha, vanilla, lemon zest, and sugar. Whip with an electric mixer on high until the mixture becomes completely smooth, light, and whippy.

ASSEMBLE THE PARFAITS

Crumble about half the cooled shortbread cookies. Assemble the parfaits in 6-ounce glasses or jars, layering crumbled cookies, then berries, then matcha coconut cream, repeating at least twice. Top with lemon zest and an extra whole shortbread cookie, for dipping and scooping.

nota bene: Both the jasmine green tea and the matcha powder in this recipe contain caffeine, so you may feel an extra jolt post-parfait.

Jasmine Cacao Nib Ice Cream with Dark Chocolate Magic Shell

When I moved out of San Francisco, I left a group of the closest girlfriends I'd had in years, which also meant leaving behind a lot of the weekly real talk about sex and the stock market and all of the other things ladies discuss when left to their own devices. I immersed myself in my new life in Los Angeles, and as Kale & Caramel grew, my network of friends began to grow across the interwebs. In my second year here, an angel named Alana came into my life via the magic of Instagram.

Instagram might as well be online dating for blogger friends, and I developed a friend crush on Alana by way of her gorgeous blog. It took a few weeks, but in a cosmic rush of excitement, we realized that we had, in point of fact, grown up ten minutes from each other on Maui, one of the most isolated islands in the world. It was kismet.

Alana and her boyfriend, Moses (and their sweet miniature dachshund, Vienna), moved to LA from San Francisco shortly thereafter, and we became fast friends. Alana taught me a million things about photography and inspired me with her kitchen prowess and introduced me to a coterie of other bloggers who quickly became some of my best friends. On top of it all, she was the kindest, most generous reminder of home that a girl in a big concrete jungle could want.

Last spring, Alana and I spent weeks foraging fresh jasmine and taste-testing a collaboration in matcha and jasmine macaron ice cream sandwiches. We forged our friendship in the perfection of crumbling French cookies and melting ice cream.

This simplified version of the ice cream we made that day features jasmine tea and an easy dark chocolate magic shell. Because, without fail, jasmine always delivers the magic.

makes 1 quart

preparation time: overnight ice cream maker freeze + 35 minutes + 8 to 9 hours chill time

JASMINE CACAO NIB ICE CREAM

2½ cups heavy cream

1½ cups whole milk

½ cup honey

¼ cup loose-leaf jasmine green tea

2 egg yolks

¼ cup raw cacao nibs

DARK CHOCOLATE MAGIC SHELL

¼ cup raw virgin coconut oil, melted

¼ cup raw cacao or cocoa powder

¼ cup semisweet chocolate chips or chunks

Pinch of vanilla seeds scraped from the pod, or
¼ teaspoon pure vanilla extract

PREPARE YOUR ICE CREAM MAKER

The night before you plan to make the ice cream, freeze the bowl of your ice cream maker.

MAKE THE ICE CREAM

In a large saucepan over medium heat, whisk the heavy cream, milk, and honey until steam rises. Add the tea, immersing it in the liquid to allow the leaves to release their oils. Cover the pan, remove from the heat, and let steep for 10 to 15 minutes, depending on how strong a flavor you want, then strain out the tea.

In a small bowl, whisk the egg yolks with ½ cup of the cream mixture, then gradually whisk the mixture back into the pan. Return to the stove, and cook over low heat, stirring continuously, until the custard reaches 170°F, 20 to 25 minutes—or until it thickens slightly and coats the back of a spoon. Transfer to an airtight container, and cool completely in the fridge.

Once chilled, freeze in the ice cream maker, according to the manufacturer's instructions, adding the cacao nibs in the last 5 minutes of churning. Pour the frozen ice cream into a freezer-safe pan or dish and freeze for at least 6 hours before eating.

No ice cream maker? The results won't be as refined, but follow the process on page 38.

MAKE THE MAGIC SHELL

Nestle a heatproof bowl into a small saucepan filled with 1 to 2 inches of water (the water should not touch the bottom of the bowl). Place the oil, cacao, chocolate chips, and vanilla in the bowl, and turn the heat to medium-high. Bring the water to a boil, stirring the ingredients continuously as they melt. Once the water boils, reduce the heat to low and continue to stir until almost all the ingredients are melted.

Remove from the heat, and whisk the mixture until smooth and velvety. Keep warm until ready to use. Drizzle over served ice cream and watch a chocolate shell magically form.

Keep in an airtight container, out of direct sunlight, for up to 1 week. The magic shell will harden at room temperature; to melt, immerse the container in hot water.

Fresh Jasmine Honey

In the spring, I track jasmine like a hound, sniffing it around street corners and following the slightest trace of scent to its source. It's been many years since I've had a patch of jasmine to call my own, so I rely on generous blossom donations from neighbors and bountiful spills of vine onto public property to sate my jasmine thirst. This past spring, though, I came across the mother lode: a stand of jasmine so rich with blossoms that I could pick handful after handful and not even recognize any were missing.

The jasmine patch was on the sweet soil of Wattles Farm Community Garden, impeccably tended by a beautiful woman named Toby. Toby had been a member of the farm for decades, and in her role as head garden master she shared with me as much jasmine as I wanted. I had reverberations of simple syrups and other infusions in my head, but the idea of jasmine honey was overpowering.

My hands drenched with morning dew, I plucked as many blossom-rich vines as I could, filling bag after bag with clouds of scent. Once I returned home, the process was stunningly simple: Clean the flowers, add them to warmed honey, and let them steep as long as I liked. A few days later, I returned with a jar of fresh jasmine honey for Toby and her family. She immediately popped off the lid and dipped her pinky finger in to take a taste. Her eyelids fluttered closed and a soft moan escaped her lips. *Yes!* she exclaimed. *Yes. Oh, yes.*

I have a feeling this is the ideal way to eat jasmine honey: without utensils, straight from the jar. That said, I recommend it anywhere and everywhere you'd typically use honey. It's delightful against the clean palate of yogurts, creams, and cheeses, and paired with fresh fruit or tea.

makes 1 cup
preparation time: 10 to 15 minutes + 2 hours + infusion time

---

1 cup filtered honey (not raw, should be runny)

2 cups fresh, clean jasmine flowers (stems and leaves discarded)

Fill a small saucepan with 2 inches of water, and nestle a small, heatproof bowl over the top to create a double boiler. The water should not touch the bottom of the bowl. Bring the water to a boil.

Add the honey to the bowl, and stir. When the honey is completely liquid and hot to the touch, add the jasmine flowers. Fold in gently and remove from the heat. Let steep for at least 2 hours in the pan (or up to 1 week in an airtight container in the fridge), then warm to liquid again and strain out the flowers. Store the honey in an airtight jar.

Jasmine Cucumber Water (Vegan)

Here are some things you can do with jasmine cucumber water:

1. Put it in a pitcher and keep it by your desk to feel like you are sipping on the liquid equivalent of a Pablo Neruda poem every ten minutes or so.
2. Put some in a spray bottle and keep in your fridge to spritz yourself when things are getting too hot to handle, psychologically, emotionally, or physically.
3. Sip on it after a workout, to feel like you've just returned to your exquisitely appointed Grecian villa after an early morning horseback ride along the shores of Santorini.
4. Strain out the cucumber, put it in a spray bottle, and keep in your boudoir for after-sex spritzing.
5. Pour some in a small bowl and float fresh jasmine or other blossoms in it for an extra fragrant reminder of ease.
6. Pour some in a small bowl, pretend that it's holy water, and douse everyone in your immediate vicinity with it, proclaiming that they are now healed.
7. Drink out of goblets (some call these "wineglasses") at the end of a luxurious meal, savoring each sip like it's nectar collected by hummingbirds from individual jasmine blossoms.
8. Invent your own jasmine cucumber water drinking game, preferably involving making out.

makes 1 quart
preparation time: 5 minutes

4 cups water

2 cups fresh, clean jasmine flowers (stems and leaves discarded)

½ cup thinly sliced cucumber rounds

Place the water, jasmine flowers, and cucumber rounds in a large mason jar and seal. Shake gently about 10 times to combine. Refrigerate until chilled as desired, and sip all day, using a straw to avoid the blossoms and cucumbers. Refill with water as many times as you like, for 48 hours. Then discard and refresh the ingredients.

Jasmine Facial Oil, Two Ways

I've never been one for facials. A part of that is my frugality—I've always worked for myself, which means constant vigilance on my budgets and bank accounts, and not a lot of whimsical spending. I loved the idea of facials, but I could never seem to justify the cost. Thank goodness, though, for my sweet friends Evan and Danielle, who treated me to a luxurious birthday facial many years ago with a brilliant Israeli woman named Anat. Anat was no-nonsense, a huge sweetheart, and convinced that I would meet my husband on my first trip to our tribe's ancestral homeland. I was into it.

Anat also delivered to me a few key skincare secrets that transformed my life for years to come. It boiled down to this: Stop using unnecessarily complex products on your skin when all it needs is gentle cleansing and hydration. What a revelation. Anat reinforced my inclination to simplicity, and then some. I threw away all my cleansers in favor of raw honey (more on that in the next chapter) and began making my own facial moisturizer in the form of an oil much like this one.

These two variations on a theme cover both drier and oilier complexions, and you can alternate between them as your skin goes through seasonal changes. Rose is extra gentle on dry, tender cheeks. Sandalwood is just slightly astringent, perfect for an oilier complexion.

nota bene: If you tend to have oily skin, your epidermis is likely overproducing oil to compensate for dryness. Give it what it needs, and it'll balance naturally. (And of course, if you have persistent skin distress of any kind you should see a dermatologist.)

makes 8 ounces
preparation time: 5 minutes

FOR NORMAL TO DRY COMPLEXIONS	FOR NORMAL TO OILY COMPLEXIONS
8 ounces sweet almond oil	8 ounces sweet almond oil
¼ cup dried edible rose petals, or 2 drops rose essential oil	4 drops jasmine essential oil
4 drops jasmine essential oil	4 drops sandalwood essential oil

For Normal to Dry Complexions, if infusing rose petals into oil: In a small saucepan, heat the almond oil over low heat, stirring continuously, until it is very hot but no bubbles form. Do not let it boil or even simmer. Add the rose petals and continue to stir, gently massaging the petals into the oil. Remove from the heat. Let cool completely. Pour into a jar and cover with a lid.

Let sit overnight. Strain through a fine-mesh strainer, cheesecloth, or tea bag and pour the oil back into the jar. Add the jasmine essential oil. Seal and shake 50 to 100 times to incorporate. Keep in a cool place, out of sunlight.

For Normal to Dry Complexions, if using rose essential oil, and for Normal to Oily Complexions: Pour the almond oil into a jar and add the jasmine and sandalwood essential oils. Seal and shake 50 to 100 times to incorporate. Keep in a cool place, out of sunlight.

Apply a dime-size amount to face after cleansing, before bed.

11

ROSE

I STOOD, ROOTED TO THAT TERRIBLE PATCH of grassless earth where he had broken up with me, and I began to notice dust motes and trees and people orbiting slowly around the centripetal force of my sadness. I felt my fingers open and close, the palms sweaty. I noticed little brown insects dodging into and out of the sun. I noticed I was barely breathing. I noticed that all I wanted to do was lie down.

I collapsed onto the ground as the tears came, the final weight of his decision to leave. Not knowing where else to go, I let my sadness pour into the dirt and the ants and the weeds. I felt safe there, or at least sure that nothing could knock me down even farther than I was. In the days that followed, I turned to small rituals to keep me sane, to keep my heart safe. I turned to rose.

The velvety lushness of rose is burdened with clichéd notions of old-fashioned romance and other snooze-worthy Victorianisms. Up close, however, rose as a scent and taste is soothing, transcendent, and calming—a balm for the heart.

To drink rose, then, or to ingest its petals, becomes an act of surrender to a moment of calm. Rose demands that you stop. That you breathe. That you feel. Sweetness and sorrow may be dislodged from the calcified tracts of emotional busyness that define daily life for most of us.

Turn to rose when you need a shot of true romance—the kind that sustains body, heart, and soul.

Discover more of rose's properties on page 171.

Cumin & Rose Roasted Cauliflower with Vinegar-Soaked Currants

I spent the second half of my twenties in a state of disbelief: My heart had been broken just days before my mother was diagnosed with cancer, and within a year and a half, she was dead. The entirety of my life as I knew it had dissolved. Nothing looked the same. Echoing within me was a deep, resounding thud of no. No to the heartbreak, no to the death, no to the trauma of change.

At my core, I was terrified. Nothing was the way I thought it would be. I did not have the partner I had dreamed of. I did not have the family I had known.

It took years for me to realize that there was something else that needed to die in order for me to live, and to live freely: the story I'd told about who I was for two and a half decades. It was old, defunct, and jagged, its weight preventing me from living the rest of my life. I towed my past and my imagined future along with me everywhere, until its strain fomented a hot anger in my belly. The only way forward was to let go, firmly, of the ideas I'd carried for so long. Finally, to accept the possibility of the new.

For the bittersweetness of change, here is a savory dish piqued with a homemade *ras el hanout* (a traditional North African spice mix) of rose petals, cardamom, cumin, and spices. Vinegar-soaked currants. The taste of letting go.

nota bene: You'll be making a larger batch of ras el hanout than required in the recipe. Store it in an airtight container in your pantry, and use on other roasted veggies, toasts, cheeses, and savory delights of your liking.

serves 4
preparation time: 40 minutes

RAS EL HANOUT

1 tablespoon plus 2 teaspoons dried edible rose petals

2 teaspoons ground cinnamon

2 teaspoons ground cumin

1 teaspoon ground cardamom

1 teaspoon freshly cracked black pepper

1 teaspoon ground allspice

ROASTED CAULIFLOWER

¼ cup red wine vinegar

3 tablespoons dried currants, plus more for garnish

1 medium head cauliflower (about 1½ pounds), washed and cut into florets

¼ cup olive oil

1 teaspoon sea salt

1 teaspoon dried edible rose petals, for garnish

Plain yogurt, to taste, for garnish

MAKE THE RAS EL HANOUT

In a clean spice grinder, coffee grinder, herb mill, or small food processor, grind the rose petals to a fine texture. Mix with the cinnamon, cumin, cardamom, pepper, and allspice and store in an airtight container.

MAKE THE CAULIFLOWER

Preheat the oven to 425°F. Line a large rimmed baking sheet with parchment paper.

Heat the vinegar and currants in a small saucepan over low heat, stirring until they become soft and plump. Set aside, reserving the vinegar for the cauliflower.

Spread the cauliflower on the baking sheet in an even layer and drizzle with the oil. Sprinkle with the salt and 1 tablespoon of the ras el hanout, and toss to coat.

Use a slotted spoon to scoop the currants from the vinegar and sprinkle 2 tablespoons of the currants over the cauliflower. Drizzle 2 tablespoons of the vinegar from the currants over the veggies. Toss again. Roast for 25 to 30 minutes, turning with a spatula halfway through, until the cauliflower is tender and browning at the edges. In the final 5 minutes of roasting, add the remaining 1 tablespoon vinegar-soaked currants and toss, then return to the oven. Serve immediately, garnished with the rose petals, additional currants, and yogurt, as desired.

Peach & Pistachio Galettes with Rose Whipped Cream

When I began to rewrite the blueprint of the life I thought I'd live, I plunged back into the one true thing I'd always known: writing. I might not know who I was, or how to make myself feel a sense of belonging or family, but I did know that writing would always be a kind of home to me. One year after my mother's death, I met author Rebecca Walker. In her master class on memoir, I discovered that it was extraordinarily difficult for me to tell the truth. To be real, not just on principle, but in my own heart. To be utterly and truly honest.

Over the years, I'd learned to hide for a number of reasons: out of fear that I would not be accepted; out of laziness, as it's much easier to believe what is convenient than what is real; and out of the sheer terror of feeling fully. I dwelled in platitudes and the glossy positive thinking of the New Age world. But then I began to write, and, with Rebecca, to excavate the real matter of loss and grief that held me captive. I thrilled to the rush of telling the truth, of not holding myself back or contorting any part of who I was. There is no solvent like the truth.

Except, perhaps, this intoxicating combination of ripe summer peach, vanilla bean, cardamom, pistachio, and rose. These mini galettes are the truthiest dessert around.

makes 5 mini galettes
preparation time: about 1 hour 35 minutes

PASTRY CRUST

1¼ cups pastry flour, plus more for rolling

2 tablespoons plus 1 teaspoon granulated sugar

¼ teaspoon sea salt

8 tablespoons (1 stick) salted butter, chilled

2 to 3 tablespoons ice water

1 egg (for the egg wash)

PISTACHIO FILLING

¾ cup shelled pistachio nuts, minced

2 tablespoons honey

¼ teaspoon vanilla seeds scraped from the pod, or ½ teaspoon pure vanilla extract

2 pinches flaky sea salt

PEACH FILLING

1 large peach, or 2 small, sliced ¼ inch thick

2 teaspoons fresh lemon juice

¼ teaspoon ground cardamom

¼ teaspoon vanilla seeds scraped from the pod, or ½ teaspoon pure vanilla extract

1 teaspoon granulated sugar

ROSE WHIPPED CREAM

1 cup chilled heavy cream

2½ teaspoons honey, or more to taste

¼ teaspoon ground cardamom

¼ teaspoon rose water, or more to taste

MAKE THE CRUST

At least 30 minutes in advance, make the pastry crust. Mix the 1¼ cups pastry flour, the sugar, and salt in a bowl. Cut the butter into small pieces (or grate it) and use a pastry cutter or fork to work it into the flour mixture until it's almost fully incorporated. Add 2 tablespoons of the ice water (you can add more later if need be) and work the dough together for just a few moments more until it is smooth and cohesive. Add another ½ to 1 tablespoon ice water if it's too dry or crumbly. Separate into 5 equal balls, gently flatten each into a ½-inch-thick disk, and cover in plastic wrap. Place in the fridge. In a small bowl, lightly beat the egg. Set it aside in the fridge until ready to use.

MAKE THE PISTACHIO FILLING

Combine the pistachios, honey, vanilla, and salt in a bowl and mix thoroughly. Set aside.

MAKE THE PEACH FILLING

Place the peaches in a bowl, and douse with the lemon juice, cardamom, vanilla, and sugar. Toss lightly just to coat, and set aside while you roll out your pastry.

ASSEMBLE THE GALETTE

Preheat the oven to 400°F. Lightly dust two baking sheet-sized pieces of parchment paper with flour. When the dough has chilled for at least 30 minutes, remove all 5 disks from the fridge and divide them between the sheets of parchment paper (the dough will stay on this parchment paper for baking). Roll each disk about ¼ inch thick, and transfer the parchment paper to the baking sheets. Distribute the pistachio filling in a small circle at the center of each disk of dough, about 2 tablespoons each, leaving a 2- to 3-inch perimeter. Reserve extra for garnish.

Layer the peaches in a circle, about 5 slices per galette, laying them flat so that each one slightly overlaps the next. Fold in the edges of the dough, layering and pinching sections together to seal any gaps (and prevent leaking). Brush the exposed dough with the egg wash. Repeat for each galette.

Place the baking sheets on middle racks, and bake for 30 to 35 minutes (rotating the baking sheet placement halfway through, and checking at 30 minutes to estimate the remaining baking time), until the peach tips are slightly brûléed, the pastry is golden brown, and the bottom is starting to caramelize.

MAKE THE WHIPPED CREAM

Just before serving, pour the heavy cream into a large bowl and add the honey, cardamom, and rose water. Whip with an electric mixer just until soft peaks form. Spoon some of the rose whipped cream atop each galette, and garnish with extra pistachio filling.

Chocolate Chia Mousse with Cardamom Rose Coco Whip (Vegan)

One day in 2011, summer in San Francisco, I decided to learn to ride the bike again. The day was green and full, the sun so hot that it burned my legs, leaving my skin to peel off in long, thin strips in the weeks to come. But before that cellular death of the person I used to be, there was just the simple desire to ride again, and the unique constellation of friends and sunshine and possibility that made the desire real.

One friend in particular, a force named Savannah, solidified that sense of possibility. Savannah skyrocketed into my life, playing field hockey, wearing silk blazers and yellow topaz, and drinking hot fudge straight from the dinner table carafe. She gathered light around her as she moved, a quickening of air and ideas that galvanized action.

That day, Savannah and a gaggle of other ladies helped me up, steadied me, and ushered me forth, full of champagne and strawberries and the sun that kissed my thighs with such intensity that later they blistered in remembrance. I rode on roughshod asphalt toward a cluster of dark trees and picnickers and babies and marigolds as Savannah and the others stood back and cheered, temporary fearlessness eating up the safety of my limitation.

If we'd had it then, we would've eaten spoonful after spoonful of this nearly raw, effortlessly light chocolate chia mousse in celebration, emboldened by the sky and the willingness to be made anew. Eat it now, in the comfort of your own home. Be new.

makes about 6 servings
preparation time: 3 to 4 hours, including chilling time

CHOCOLATE CHIA MOUSSE

¾ cup chia seeds

⅓ cup plus 1 tablespoon cocoa powder

2 pinches sea salt

2¼ cups (nut) milk of choice

¼ cup plus 1½ tablespoons pure maple syrup

½ teaspoon pure vanilla extract

1½ cups semisweet chocolate chips

1 teaspoon orange zest

⅛ teaspoon ground cardamom

CARDAMOM ROSE COCO WHIP

1 (13.5-ounce) can full-fat coconut milk,
   refrigerated upside down

2 tablespoons confectioners' sugar

¼ teaspoon rose water

¼ teaspoon ground cardamom

MOUSSE TOPPINGS

¼ cup cacao nibs

1 tablespoon dried edible rose petals
   (stems and leaves discarded)

MAKE THE MOUSSE

At least 1 hour before serving, combine the chia seeds, cocoa powder, and salt in a large bowl. Whisk to combine. Add your milk of choice, maple syrup, and vanilla and continue whisking until all cocoa powder clumps are dissolved and the chia begins to thicken. Cover with plastic wrap and place in the fridge for at least 1 hour, or as long as overnight.

Transfer the thickened chocolate chia pudding to a blender and blend on high until very creamy and smooth. In a double boiler over boiling water, melt the chocolate chips until the chocolate is completely smooth.

Add the melted chocolate, orange zest, and cardamom to the blender with the blended chia pudding, and blend on low until all is incorporated. Taste and add a touch more sweetness or salt if you like. Scoop the mousse out of the blender and into a bowl. Refrigerate for 2 to 3 hours, to set.

MAKE THE COCO WHIP

Open the bottom of the can of chilled coconut milk, scoop out the thick coconut cream, and discard the rest of the liquid. In a large bowl, mix the coconut cream with the sugar, rose water, and cardamom. Whip with an electric mixer on high until the mixture becomes smooth, light, and whippy.

Top the mousse with cardamom rose coco whip and sprinkle with the cacao nibs and rose petals.

Pink Grapefruit, Cucumber & Rose Skin Quencher (Vegan)

My friend Liba and I share many things: a shoe size—which means we have, in recent years, taken to exchanging and curating a shared collection—a love of holding hands, an obsession with phở, a keen appreciation for rituals of remembrance and spirit, and, most important, a propensity to surround ourselves with beverages of all kinds. Beginning in college, we'd arm ourselves with a selection of teas, juices, sparkling and flavored waters, and lattes, just for one meal. There was something luxurious about it, something reassuring. If we knew nothing else, we knew we would not go thirsty. Hydrated ladies that we are, to this day we can be found snuggling over brunch with copious fluids in near reach.

Liba has also been the willing and eager subject of many a Kale & Caramel experiment, both in the kitchen and for the body. And so, as she has recently become a mother, I wanted to make her a juice for self-protection, for hydration, a tonic that would nourish her mind and her heart and her skin. Made with pink grapefruit plucked from her and her husband's garden, it doesn't get much sunnier.

Pink grapefruit contains high levels of vitamin C, cucumber floods the body with anti-inflammatories, and rose soothes both cellularly and subcellularly. The antioxidants in this glass will fuel you for days, brightening your skin and your spirit. This is serious power food, drenched in mellow, sensual loveliness.

serves 2

preparation time: about 10 minutes

3 small pink grapefruits, or 2 large

5-inch length of cucumber, peeled and chopped (about 1 cup)

¼ teaspoon rose water, or to taste

4 to 5 ice cubes

Stevia or sweetener of choice (such as maple syrup or honey), optional, to taste

Remove the skin, seeds, and membranes of the grapefruits (the membranes can be very bitter, so make sure to remove them as best as possible). You should have about 2 cups of peeled grapefruit sections.

Starting with the grapefruit, place the cucumber, rose water, ice, and stevia in a blender. Blend on high until fully incorporated. Taste, and add more rose water if desired. If it tastes slightly bitter (grapefruits may vary in their sweetness), you can add a few drops of stevia and blend to mix.

Pour. Ahhh.

MAKE IT A COCKTAIL!
Vodka, St. Germain, gin.

Watermelon Rose Elixir (Vegan)

It was the first time I said no to you. No, you could not have us both; no, I would not wait. No, you could not have my body while some of you was still with her. No. Just, simply, no. And then it was as though I could see you for the first time. You turned cold and ugly. Then, when you should have cried, there was nothing. I drove back to LA and smashed a dozen wineglasses, carefully wrapped in paper and plastic so they wouldn't make a mess, with a hammer.

I grieved.

Tending to a broken heart is the work of the hopeful and the patient, and also the ruthless—more than anything else, there must survive a ruthless belief that out of the hurt and the anger there will come a truer, better love.

I am a master of broken hearts. I know their heft, their listlessness, their snot, and their rage. But I believe. I still believe.

And as much internal work and psyche cleansing and self-protecting as we do, there are also tonics for the heart that help, from the outside in. Watermelon juice replenishes lost tears, and rose melds perfectly with the tender pink flesh to heal and uplift. This is love, true and clean.

serves 2

preparation time: 5 minutes

About 4 cups chilled fresh watermelon cubes

¼ to ½ teaspoon rose water, plus more to taste

3 to 4 ice cubes, cracked

3 to 4 drops stevia or other sweetener (optional)

Place the watermelon, rose water, ice, and stevia in a blender and mix until fully incorporated. Enjoy, preferably near some sweet-smelling flowers.

MAKE IT A COCKTAIL!
Vodka, St. Germain, gin, champagne.

Honey Rose Facial Cleanser

When I first tell people that I wash my face with honey, they don't always believe me. It seems too good and far too simple to be true. Don't we need complex acids, skin conditioners, and anti-inflammatories to get glowing skin? Don't we need to spend an excessive amount of money to get excessively beautifying results?

Absolutely not. Anat, the aesthetician I mentioned earlier, recommended this treatment to me nearly ten years ago, after I told her I was using a facial cleanser that was far too abrasive for my sensitive skin. Honey is a miracle worker, acting as an antibacterial, pore cleanser, and preservative (read: anti-aging tour de force). Washing my face with honey has become one of my favorite daily routines, both because it's a sensual delight, and because my skin feels so good after I use it.

I add rose here to reduce skin irritation, act as an antiseptic, and to diminish the appearance of scars and acne. It's also a nerve tonic and aphrodisiac. The combination ensures you'll walk away from your daily face-wash feeling super groovy.

Make sure you buy raw, unfiltered honey for these purposes. If I can't get raw, unfiltered honey at the farmers' market, I buy the jars sold by Whole Foods or Trader Joe's. This is critical because raw, unfiltered honey has a granular texture that doubles as a gentle exfoliator.

This recipe is for dry or normal skin. For oilier skin, add a touch of lemon juice.

nota bene: If you're exposed to sun directly after using citrus on skin, you may experience severe burning or irritation. Make sure to wash your skin well after application, wait at least several hours before exposing yourself to the sun, and always apply sunscreen for protection. Moreover, excessive use of citrus on skin can cause lightening, so don't use citrus more than once a week.

makes 2 to 3 weeks' worth, depending on frequency of use
preparation time: 5 minutes

1 to 2 tablespoons dried edible rose petals (stems and leaves discarded)

¼ cup raw honey
A touch of lemon juice (for oilier skin types only)

Grind the rose petals in a clean spice grinder, coffee grinder, herb mill, or small food processor until they're small flecks and dust. For greater exfoliation, use more petals and leave them in larger flecks. Transfer to a small bowl and add the honey and the lemon juice, if using, and stir to integrate the petals.

Splash face with water, then apply ½ teaspoon or more of the honey rose mixture. Massage in circles around face and neck, adding extra force for deeper exfoliation. Wash completely with water and moisturize (with Jasmine Facial Oil, page 204).

Cucumber Rose Petal Mask

Where some venture into their refrigerators to find mealtime fixings, I often scout the shelves for skincare ingredients. Citrus brightens; papaya activates; melons, peaches and nectarines deliver mild doses of fruit acid; and greens tone the epidermis. And, here, cucumber hydrates and yogurt softens.

The more I relate to my fridge as a source of inner and outer nourishment, the more fun it is for me to be in my kitchen. And on nights when I need a quick solution for some TLC, a fridge forage often yields unexpectedly beautiful results. Combining simple, food-based ingredients with floral companions like rose elevates the experimentation without complicating the process.

This cucumber rose petal mask is the perfect excuse to check out for an evening, to soothe your skin, your heart, and your frazzled nerves. Cucumber nourishes, yogurt gently soothes and exfoliates, and rose (two ways) nurtures from the outside in.

Let this easy mask be your excuse to dive into the deep quiet of rose and the fresh perfume of cucumber. Emerge glowing.

makes enough for 3 to 4 uses
preparation time: 15 minutes

½ cup finely grated peeled cucumber

2 tablespoons dried edible rose petals (stems and leaves discarded)

¼ teaspoon rose water

2 tablespoons plain yogurt (optional)

Place the cucumber in a fine mesh sieve or in cheesecloth and squeeze out as much liquid as possible. Place the drained cucumber with the rose petals, rose water, and yogurt, if using, in a small bowl, and stir to combine. Cover, and let sit in the fridge for about 10 minutes to allow the rose petals to soften.

Blend in a small food processor or blender until smooth. Use about 1 tablespoon per application, and smooth onto clean skin in an even layer. Leave on for 5 to 10 minutes, then rinse off. Dry face and moisturize with Jasmine Facial Oil (page 204).

12

ORANGE BLOSSOM

MAUI GIRL THAT I AM, California will always be my first home. Born on the cliffs of the tiny town of Bolinas, I am completely and utterly smitten with the scope and the beauty of the state, its seismic shimmer, its heat and mossy green, its parched desert and vibrant sierra. Though I only lived in Bolinas the first two years of my life, my choice to move to San Francisco, and later to Los Angeles, was my passageway to adulthood. For the first time, I lived alone. For the first time, I had to seek out my own wildness within an otherwise tame urban landscape.

I quickly found pockets of wild everywhere, on city blocks, in friends' backyards, at the community farm, in the modest courtyard of my own apartment building. To wild myself meant to remember where I'd seen hibiscus, where roses were nodding their buds open to the sun, where orange blossoms were falling, heavy with scent, on the sidewalk. My mind created these constellations of sensual memory as a map of self-remembrance. Knowing where to find rosemary and lavender at my farmers' market—and on my block—let me breathe easier.

And, every spring, there was orange blossom—the sweetest yes of them all, the wildest in spirit and scent. Orange blossom calms and soothes, it sings arias of ease and sex and nourishment, it reminds of the fullness of possibility, the coming of fruit.

Discover more of orange blossom's properties on page 171.

Carrot, Feta & Pistachio Salad with Orange Blossom Toss

Somewhere along the way, I decided that if I couldn't surprise myself at least once a day, I was doing it wrong. I wanted to feel alive, to prove to myself that I was capable of change. This commitment took many forms: cutting off fifteen inches of hair, eating food that scared me, going to restaurants alone, having vulnerable and honest conversations that summoned my most grown-up self, and starting my own business. And, one evening on Maui, it took the form of a group of friends and me deciding to have a naked dinner party.

I'd arrived early to help our hosts, Ashana and Ryan, cook. Evan and Danielle came shortly thereafter, and somehow the topic turned to Yale's infamous naked parties, of which I'd only attended one. Someone jokingly suggested we have a naked dinner party, and suddenly, with a shift in the air, it was no longer a joke. I turned to put something in the sink, and Ashana's clothes were off. Soon Ryan's were, too, and then Evan's and Danielle's. And mine. We began laughing hysterically at the absurdity of it all, and at how surprised Gabby, Bennett, and Sarah would be when they arrived.

Stepping through the doorway, Bennett began taking off his clothes even before he knew what was going on. He was a shoo-in, as he'd started a naked club in his neighborhood as a child. Gabby and Sarah abstained, but there was something easeful and charming about it all. Soon, I forgot I was naked. And it was only when the evening breeze picked up and I realized certain, ahem, parts of my body were quite chilly that I remembered there was a thing called clothing that I could use to cover myself.

This salad is an ode to surprise, a play on more traditional Middle Eastern flavors, which often weave orange blossom into savory dishes as a way to elevate the intensity of spices and meats. Here, with sweet and earthy raw carrot, it is an ode to friends who will do the unexpected, to flavors that elicit freedom.

serves 4 to 6

preparation time: about 15 minutes

ORANGE BLOSSOM TOSS

2 tablespoons olive oil

3 tablespoons red wine vinegar

1½ teaspoons orange blossom water

2 teaspoons honey

¼ teaspoon ground cumin

¼ teaspoon ground cardamom

¼ teaspoon crushed red pepper flakes, plus more for garnish

¼ teaspoon sea salt

CARROT, FETA, AND PISTACHIO SALAD

10 carrots, washed and tops trimmed and reserved

1 cup coarsely chopped fresh mint leaves, plus more for garnish

⅔ cup chopped toasted pistachio nuts

⅔ cup crumbled feta cheese

MAKE THE ORANGE BLOSSOM TOSS

Combine the oil, vinegar, orange blossom water, honey, cumin, cardamom, the ¼ teaspoon red pepper flakes, and the salt in a jar, seal, and shake to blend. Alternately, whisk the ingredients in a small bowl and set aside.

MAKE THE SALAD

Use a vegetable peeler, mandoline, or spiralizer to slice the carrots into long, thin strips. Finely chop a handful of carrot tops (resulting in about ¼ cup). Place the carrot strips and carrot tops in a large salad bowl.

Add the mint and pistachios, and pour the dressing over all. Toss to combine. Gently fold in the feta. Top with mint and extra red pepper flakes, if you want an additional kick of spice.

Orange Blossom Pistachio Milk

Sometimes when I'm making a new salad or smoothie, fruit crisp or lentil loaf, my first thought is a wish that my mother could taste it. I often wonder if I can communicate with her—gone though she is—even more seamlessly by spirit than by body. Could she somehow taste this pistachio milk, if I summoned her to me, to it? Could she smell the orange blossom and teach me the many ways orange blossom soothes the system?

Could I whisper to her all the other things she's missed and ask her what she thinks of the person I've become?

Growing up, I see this longing as, in part, me wanting to know myself, to say yes to myself, as I am now, without her. But I still like to think she might see some of these delicate creations, see herself in them, see the beauty of what she taught me. Taste the orange blossom laced through the pistachio.

Orange blossom is, for me, the way to spirit conversations rooted here on earth.

And as for this milk, I gasped when I took my first sip of it—it's that ethereally delicious. It's perfect on its own, or with fruit, over ice cream, in a milk shake, as the base for a chia or tapioca pudding, with tea, or heated and frothed as a nut milk steamer.

nota bene: If you can't find unsalted pistachio nuts, simply give the salted pistachio nuts a few very good rinses before and after soaking, and omit the additional salt.

makes about 3 cups
preparation time: overnight soak + 20 minutes

½ cup shelled unsalted pistachio nuts, ideally raw though roasted is okay

3 cups water for soaking, plus 2½ cups water for blending

2 to 3 tablespoons honey

¼ teaspoon vanilla seeds scraped from the pod, or ½ teaspoon pure vanilla extract

⅛ teaspoon ground cardamom

2 pinches sea salt

1 teaspoon orange blossom water, plus more to taste

SOAK THE NUTS

The night before you want to make the milk, soak the nuts in the 3 cups water. The next day, or after soaking for at least 8 hours, squeeze the pistachio meats out of their purplish-brown casings (this is for the sake of color and texture, but can be skipped if you're in a hurry). Discard the casings, and rinse the soft, green nut meats.

MAKE THE MILK

Place the pistachios in a high-powered blender with the 2½ cups water. Blend on high until all is completely smooth, 1 to 2 minutes. Pour through a nut milk bag, or other fine straining tool, squeezing to remove every last drop of liquid from the pistachio pulp.

Return the milk to the (rinsed) blender, and add the honey, vanilla, cardamom, salt, and orange blossom water. Blend to incorporate, about 30 seconds. Taste (perhaps gasp, as I did) and adjust the sweetness and orange blossom water as you like.

Fig & Orange Blossom Yogurt Tarts

There was a burbling fountain and a giant stand of rosemary and a fig tree so flush with fruit that in the summer the beetles took up permanent residence in the fleshy, jammy orbs. There was a long table beautifully set, evoking the sumptuousness of my friend Suzanne's family traditions, of ritual moving into its next generation. It was my first Passover in Los Angeles. The courtyard was strung with lights and bright with friends.

In the decade Suzanne had made LA her home, she'd also discovered the necessity of creating family on a coast that was not historically her own—and she'd done so richly well. As guests fluttered in, I saw friends I'd known for years, and others who were to become close confidants. In the warmth of an LA spring evening, Suzanne served us perfect course after course. Her welcome, the insistence of rosemary and figs and warm air on skin, the laughter deepening into conversation, all of these softened Los Angeles into home.

This feast inspired me to new culinary exploration in my own kitchen and led to these sweet and simple little tarts. Serve them outdoors, on a warm evening, and let the bright sugar of fruit, the mellow cut of olive oil, and the floral reach of orange blossom weave home for you.

makes about 16 mini tarts
preparation time: about 2 hours

TART SHELLS

1¼ cups all-purpose flour, plus more for rolling

⅓ cup confectioners' sugar

½ teaspoon sea salt

¼ teaspoon ground cardamom

¼ teaspoon vanilla seeds scraped from the pod, or ½ teaspoon pure vanilla extract

5 ounces (1¼ sticks) unsalted butter, chilled and cut into small pieces

2 egg yolks, beaten

FILLING

1 tablespoon honey

½ teaspoon orange blossom water

1 cup plain Greek yogurt

6 large figs

1 large nectarine

6 sprigs fresh mint

Olive oil, for drizzling

Flaky sea salt, for garnish

MAKE THE TART SHELLS

In a medium bowl, whisk the flour, sugar, salt, cardamom, and vanilla seeds (if using vanilla extract, add later with the egg yolks). Add the butter, and mix into the dry ingredients using your fingertips or a pastry cutter, just until the butter is in pea-size pieces and beginning to make the mix a bit sandy looking. Add the egg yolks and continue to mix until the dough comes together and has a sandy texture. Divide into 2 balls and pat into even 5-inch disks. Wrap in plastic wrap and refrigerate for 1 hour.

After an hour, remove the disks of dough from the fridge and preheat the oven to 400°F. On a lightly floured surface, roll out the disks of dough one at a time to ¼-inch thickness. Use a 3-inch cookie cutter (or a 3-inch-diameter water glass, like I did!) to cut 16 circles total. Transfer each circle immediately to the base of a nonstick muffin tin or tart pan, gently pressing to ensure even contact with the bottom and sides of the pan. Feel free to consolidate and reroll the dough as you go, but remember that the closer to room temperature it gets, the more difficult it is to work with.

Bake for 15 to 20 minutes, until just golden brown. Remove from the oven and let rest on a cooling rack for at least 15 minutes. Then lift the tart shells from the tins and leave them to cool further on the rack.

MAKE THE FILLING AND ASSEMBLE THE TARTS

In a small bowl, gently swirl the honey and orange blossom water into the yogurt and place in the fridge until ready to fill the tarts. I like to leave a few ribbons of honey in the yogurt as opposed to fully mixing it in.

Slice the figs and nectarines into thin wedges and slices, respectively.

Remove the yogurt blend from the fridge and spoon evenly into the tart shells. Garnish each tart with a few fig wedges and nectarine slices. Add mint leaves liberally. Finally, drizzle with oil and add a tiny sprinkle of salt on each tart. Let rest in the fridge for 30 minutes, and serve immediately!

Coconut, Hibiscus & Blood Orange Blossom Slushies

When I am away from Maui, I miss the ocean constantly. I am in bliss under the water, immersed in the cool blue wash of salt and tide and weightlessness. My father and I released the last of my mother's ashes in this weightlessness, set them free into the plaintive, aching songs of whales in calving season. In the ocean, light filtering through wave fractals, I come home to myself.

In California, though, the ocean is different. When I lived in San Francisco, I felt acutely the lack of saltwater on my skin. And even when I first moved south to LA, where the water was a bit warmer, it was hard to imagine spending time in it as I did on Maui. In my second year in LA, I knew that had to change. The heat was tremendous, unlike any I'd experienced before—a heat that softened my brain and tired my eyes and set my body aflame. More than ever, I needed the ocean. And so I went.

I decided that the sweet relief of getting in was worth the long drive to Malibu, and I began making the pilgrimage each weekend. I went no matter the traffic, no matter the holiday; I went to flee from the 100°F-plus thermometer readings; I went to feel human again. To be baptized anew in the remembrance of my connection to the earth.

On those beach days, I'd come home full of salt and sand and breath, wanting only to feel the freshness continue. These slushies are a perennial summer floating on the sea, sweet and tangy coconut paired with lush hibiscus and orange blossom. They will transport you to the ocean, no matter where you are.

serves 2 to 4
preparation time: overnight freeze time + 40 minutes + chill time

COCONUT LIME SLUSHIE BASE

1 (13.5-ounce) can full-fat coconut milk

2 tablespoons honey

1½ teaspoons lime juice

2 pinches sea salt

HIBISCUS BLOOD ORANGE BLOSSOM SYRUP

½ cup dried hibiscus flowers

1½ cups boiling water

½ cup fresh blood orange or regular orange juice (from 2 medium oranges)

2 to 4 tablespoons honey, or to taste

⅛ teaspoon vanilla seeds scraped from the pod, or ¼ teaspoon pure vanilla extract

1½ teaspoons orange blossom water

6 to 8 ice cubes, or more as needed

THE NIGHT BEFORE: MAKE THE BASE
Shake the can of coconut milk, open, and empty the contents into a small saucepan, warming over low heat until any solids disappear. Stir in the honey, lime juice, and salt until all the ingredients are incorporated. Pour into ice cube molds and freeze until solid.

MAKE THE SYRUP
Place the hibiscus flowers in a medium heatproof bowl and pour the boiling water over the top. Let steep until the mixture reaches room temperature, then stir in the blood orange juice. Steep for at least 20 minutes and up to overnight (in a sealed container in the fridge, if overnight), then strain out the flowers.

Once the mixture has steeped, place it in a small saucepan with 2 tablespoons honey and the vanilla and bring to a boil. Simmer until reduced by half, about 20 minutes. Taste, and add more honey if desired; sweetness will vary depending on the hibiscus and citrus used. Transfer the syrup to a glass and place in the freezer or fridge to cool completely (depending on how quickly you want to use it—don't forget to take it out of the freezer, though!). When cold, stir in the orange blossom water.

MAKE THE SLUSHIES
The next day, and once the hibiscus orange blossom syrup has chilled, place all the coconut lime ice cubes with at least 6 regular water ice cubes in a high-speed blender. I like to crack ice cubes using the back of a metal spoon so they're easier to blend. You can add a little water if you're having trouble blending. If you have one, use a blender tamper to compress the cubes as they blend. The end result will be a slushie with the texture of snow or shaved ice.

Layer the slushie and hibiscus orange blossom syrup as you like—taste them together so you know the ratio you want. Drink up!

Citrus Blossom Sugar Brightening Scrub

At the end of the day, all I really want is to play with my food. The ultimate wildness is in play, in opening up to every possibility of fun and flavor and texture. Of course, this applies just as much to body and beauty experiments as it does to kitchen adventures. Which is why I had to bring you at least one entirely edible body scrub.

This skin-brightening exfoliator is made with coconut oil, sugar, citrus zests, and orange blossom water, creating a heady concoction that will leave you refreshed and inspired. The oils from citrus zest prepare the skin for exfoliation even as they awaken your mind and nervous system. As antioxidant vitamin C from the citrus works its magic to soften dead skin cells, sugar swoops in to wash everything away. Orange blossom adds mellow notes of romance and whimsy. This is the scrub to make when you want eternal summer sunshine in your heart, and a dance of light on your skin.

Yes, it is 100 percent edible. Yes, if you eat it while you're using it you may also be eating dead skin cells (your own, or anyone else's your paws are on). Yes, it'll still taste pretty darn good. Don't say you weren't warned.

nota bene: If you're exposed to sun directly after using citrus on skin, you may experience severe burning or irritation. Make sure to wash your skin well after application, wait at least several hours before exposing yourself to the sun, and always apply sunscreen for protection. Moreover, excessive use of citrus on skin can cause lightening, so don't use citrus more than once a week.

makes about 1½ cups
preparation time: 7 minutes

1 tablespoon orange zest

1 tablespoon lemon zest

1 tablespoon lemon juice

1½ cups granulated sugar

1 tablespoon melted raw virgin coconut oil

½ teaspoon orange blossom water

Combine the citrus zests, lemon juice, and sugar in a small bowl. Add the oil and stir to combine. Stir in the orange blossom water. Mix completely, then transfer to an airtight container.

Apply liberally to the body. Do not use on the face.

Store up to 1 week at room temperature, out of sunlight, or in the fridge for up to 1 month.

Full Moon Blossom Oil

It is full moon and I am home on Maui. My father and I walk the land, removing intrusive vines here and there, visiting the lychee tree where my mother's ashes are buried, talking to the plants. I let the mosquitoes eat me, not caring about the bites, happy to give them a little bit of blood for the gift of being here. Full moons have watched over many births and deaths in my life, seen mind-streams passing in the tide of the night, hearts exiting and entering the earth. This moon, though, is calm and easy. Dad pulls one last vine from a spider lily, looks to the darkening sky for some end-of-day benediction, and goes inside. I stay out.

The moon is everywhere, on mango leaves, on the strong blades of kikuyu grass that scratch my calves as I walk, on orange blossoms. It is on me, on this land that taught me to be wild, to notice the moon on my skin, my hands, my hair. It illuminates the path back to the house, where my mother used to mix oils, where my parents danced in the kitchen, where I grieved, and became new again.

I breathe in the night, as the land has taught me to do. My heart rattles the cage of my chest. My human work seems simple, in the orange-blossom breeze of full moon: To feel fully and then be free of feeling. To be free.

Here, an oil infused with orange blossom (neroli), full of the moon, of feeling, of freedom.

makes 8 ounces
preparation time: 5 minutes

8 ounces sweet almond oil
4 drops neroli essential oil

2 drops sandalwood essential oil (optional)

Pour the almond oil into a clean glass bottle and add the essential oil(s). Seal and shake 50 to 100 times to incorporate. Keep in a cool place, out of sunlight. Use as a face and body moisturizer and anointing oil. For anointing, place on pulse points of the wrists, sides and back of the neck, and over the heart.

Acknowledgments

This book exists and I am still standing thanks to the love, brilliance, and support of my agent, Nicole Tourtelot; my father, Martin Diamond; my mentor, Rebecca Walker; and the friends and family who reminded me I was never alone in the process. Tremendous thanks to Leslie Meredith, Amy Trombat, and the entire team at Atria and Simon & Schuster, for their unflagging belief in me.

Immeasurable gratitude to my recipe testers: Susan Boatright, Caterina Snyder, Casi Kneebone, Tess Hanson DeLisa, Molly Yeh, Alana Kysar, Ben Evans, Elliot Greenberger, Kira Lenke, Suryamayi Clarence-Smith, Beau Ciolino, Matt Armato, Gabby Anderman, Ashana Morrow, Brooke Bass, Wendy Levey, Sarah Klegman, Betty Liu, Janson Woodlee, Sherrie Castellano, Kristan Raines, Jennie Tucker, Tara Tucker, Renee Byrd, Alanna Taylor-Tobin, Amanda Paa, Julie Whitesell, Sara Getz, Claire Gagne, Petey Gibson, Chad Callaghan, Haley Hunt Davis, Maggie Moss-Tucker, and Suzanne Joskow. Your hands and mouths and insights are in these pages.

To my second shooters, Molly Yeh, Rachael Lee Stroud, and Rachael Kelly: thank you for capturing pure beauty.

And to Toby Leaman and the Wattles Farm community: Thank you for nurturing a true paradise in the middle of the grit, and for sharing it so generously with me.

Finally, none of this would be were it not for the beauty, love, and wisdom imparted to me by my mother, Denise Diamond (1944–2008). You told me to listen: to the breath, to the breeze, to the flowers. I still am.

Index

Page references in *italics* refer to illustrations.

D

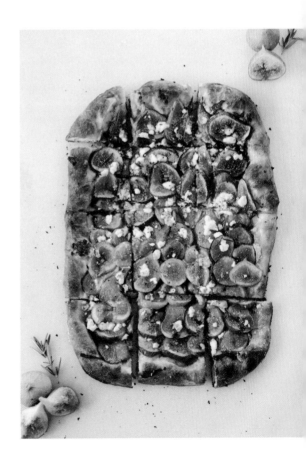